To/

Nick.

I truly wish you enjoy this Book.

Thank you, for all your help and encouragment.

Kind regards.

Mary.

GW00730573

Life Begins

when you are ready to listen

Mary Curran

BALBOA.PRESS
A DIVISION OF HAY HOUSE

Copyright © 2023 Mary Curran.

All rights reserved. No part of this book may be used or reproduced by any means, graphic, electronic, or mechanical, including photocopying, recording, taping or by any information storage retrieval system without the written permission of the author except in the case of brief quotations embodied in critical articles and reviews.

Balboa Press books may be ordered through booksellers or by contacting:

Balboa Press
A Division of Hay House
1663 Liberty Drive
Bloomington, IN 47403
www.balboapress.co.uk
UK TFN: 0800 0148647 (Toll Free inside the UK)
UK Local: (02) 0369 56325 (+44 20 3695 6325 from outside the UK)

Because of the dynamic nature of the Internet, any web addresses or links contained in this book may have changed since publication and may no longer be valid. The views expressed in this work are solely those of the author and do not necessarily reflect the views of the publisher, and the publisher hereby disclaims any responsibility for them.

The author of this book does not dispense medical advice or prescribe the use of any technique as a form of treatment for physical, emotional, or medical problems without the advice of a physician, either directly or indirectly. The intent of the author is only to offer information of a general nature to help you in your quest for emotional and spiritual well-being. In the event you use any of the information in this book for yourself, which is your constitutional right, the author and the publisher assume no responsibility for your actions.

Any people depicted in stock imagery provided by Getty Images are models, and such images are being used for illustrative purposes only. Certain stock imagery © Getty Images.

"Life begins when you are ready to listen" is Mary Curran's first book.

The day you are ready to listen – to both the inner intuitive messages as well as the outer messages - that's the day your life will change for the better.
© Mary Curran

Print information available on the last page.

ISBN: 978-1-9822-8799-3 (sc)
ISBN: 978-1-9822-8800-6 (e)

Balboa Press rev. date: 11/30/2023

Acknowledgements

· ·

This book is dedicated to my wonderful husband Andy who is my rock and support in life. A big "thank you" to my wonderful son Dion, who has provided laughter and happiness throughout my journey as a Personal and Executive Coach from the outset.

Thanks also, to my siblings and Aunt Kitty who inspired me to be grateful for everything in my life and to always hold a candle of hope for everyone.

Thanks to all my wonderful friends, fellow coaches and supervisors who have shown me the wonderful treasure of sharing, loving, and learning together.

Finally, I would like to thank Nick Williams whose book *"The work we were born to do"* and who came to Ireland to run many workshops on this subject. His inspiration, support, and encouragement along my journey through career change is the reason I am where I am today.

Contents

· ·

About Mary Curran

. . . .

Mary Curran is a Personal and Executive Coach and one of the first to set up in Ireland. She trained professionally in America in 2001 under expert Coach Thomas Leonard, graduated as a supervisor for coaches in Advanced Supervision from the University of Middlesex and is a Master Practitioner in Neuro Linguistic Programming.

In November 1999 Mary established the Centre for Professional and Personal Development in Dublin, Ireland. Over the years, in line with her core passion for 'empowering people to move from great to brilliant', she has empowered thousands of individuals to tap into their own power in order to improve their personal, professional and business lives.

As the founder of the Coach Centre in Dublin, Co-founder of the Life and Business Coaching Association of Ireland and Founding Member of the Association for Coaching, Mary has mentored and trained many of Ireland's top Coaches.

Mary specialises in business and relationship coaching, executive transition and career management, dealing with high potential career development and stepping into new roles; mid-life career change; breaking the glass ceiling and retirement planning.

Mary has appeared as a guest on TV3 am, RTE 1, "The Afternoon Show". Mary has also participated in the RTE 2FM Gerry Ryan Show and the Marion Finucane Show. She is a frequent guest speaker and motivational speaker at public events and training workshops.

Accreditations

Mary is accredited in several behavioural psychology models and psychometrics which she integrates into her coaching. These include Belbin Team Role profiling, Insights profiling and Baron EQ.

Prior to becoming a Coach, Mary had an entrepreneurial and marketing background, having set up and managed Pavlova Pantry, an Australian style restaurant business which she ran successfully for nine years and for which she won the Electricity Supply Board Innovative Business Ideas Competition in 1988.

Introduction – A Message From Mary Curran, Personal & Executive Coach

I believe you are on this earth to excel and to move from great to brilliant in every aspect of your life. You are not here to bury your talents in the ground – you are here to acknowledge that each of us is born with the potential for greatness.

The title of this book *"Life begins when you are ready to listen"* has been chosen for a reason. When you start to hear and own the messages within you, you see the gift life really is. Being open to hearing the many messages within you, is a critical part of developing your potential.

My own experiences in coaching have taught me that many people have already received insights along the way as to what their life purpose is. Clients have told me that in the past they received messages from friends, family and people close to them, who pointed out what they were good at and where their unique gifts and talents lay. However, at the time they were not ready to listen and not open to these messages, and therefore could not act upon them.

I ask you now to think about the various messages you have heard from people around you over the years, those well-intentioned words highlighting the natural gifts, talents and abilities you possess, which are your unique selling points. Have you acted on these yet?

Perhaps sometimes you were not ready to hear or listen to these messages. However, the day you *do* listen is the day your life truly begins to acknowledge your potential.

As a Personal and Executive Coach, my purpose is to empower you to be brilliant. Within the coaching relationship I seek to move you from power*less*ness to power*ful*ness by taking you on a journey to discover and develop your true potential.

If at this moment you feel that you want more from life; want greater choices and have a yearning to reach your true potential, then this book is for you. Alternatively, if you feel down; feel you do not have any choices; that you are helpless; or if you are looking for a way out and hate what you are doing but have no clue what to do about your situation; or if you are in a relationship but feel you are not being true to yourself or the other person and life is hell, then this book is for you also.

What Is Coaching?

Coaching is a three way process; The Coach, the Client and the Relationship. Coaching facilitates the performance, process of discovery and goal setting of an individual. Through the process of coaching, the client makes positive changes, with clarity and conviction.

Excelling In Your Life

It seems to be a cultural thing in Ireland that excelling in our lives is something we are afraid to even talk about. This is evident in the very language we use, where people are commonly advised not to *blow their own trumpet,* not to *count their chickens before they hatch*, not to *aim too high* for fear of disappointment.

There is also an unfortunate knock-down culture and a tendency towards begrudgery that serves to keep people *in their place.* You often hear this in general conversation when people make statements about somebody getting *too big for their boots* or being *big headed* about something.

Additionally, as human beings, there is a tendency to maximise your negatives and minimise your positives. This is particularly an Irish thing and there is a part of us afraid to be our greatest self. In my experience as a Personal & Executive Coach, this negativity is not so evident in other nationalities.

For example, a difference can be seen in the self-confidence of Continental Europeans. Many just say it as it is, and I think that is a great way to be. Whereas, in Ireland when someone speaks out, others often respond negatively. They may say something such as, *"She's very direct, isn't she?"* – A remark designed to act as a knock-back.

This culture has had a real impact on how Irish people approach their lives, and in my opinion, you are now only getting around to the idea that being the best you can be is the correct ambition to have. You are only beginning to move in this area of being confident and competent and of being able to enjoy the feeling that comes from using your abilities and fulfilling your potential.

The Growth Of Life Coaching

Twenty-three years ago, when life coaching was first introduced in Ireland, a perception arose of it being a quick-fix therapy that solved issues through counselling. Some thought that life coaches would simply offer advice over the phone and the client's problems would be sorted.

However, coaching is not counselling. Essentially coaching is about, identifying where you are now and where you want to go - and then bridging the gap in between. The transformation takes place once you have been coached on how to tap into your own natural abilities and inner potential.

Unlike therapy, coaching does not look back at events in your life with a view to figuring out why they happened, but instead, it is about learning from the past, breaking the patterns and moving forward.

When life coaching started in Ireland, people were curious but perhaps reluctant to engage with it. Over time, however, as more and more have engaged with the process, people see the changes in behaviour and attitude in those who have been coached and are becoming interested in experiencing the coaching process for themselves.

Life coaching, while still relatively new in Ireland, is now viewed as a positive and powerful process.

The business sector particularly has embraced the coaching process, and many companies now employ internal coaches who work with employees and refer employees to external coaches like myself.

Once coaching is accepted as standard practice in a company, this changes the work environment in a positive way. Instead of employees blaming colleagues for where they are, and the job they do, coaching encourages them to take personal responsibility at work and leads to a happy and productive work environment.

Businesses have experienced the real life positive impact of coaching in the workplace, and therefore embrace coaching as a most desirable part of employee development.

Coaching Is For Everyone

In terms of coaching with a view to self-actualisation- i.e., fulfilling your potential to become all that you can be- revaluating your life at various points along the way is of paramount importance. Once you start feeling stuck and unable to see outside yourself, it is time to re-evaluate.

What this means is you need to stop and take a good look to ascertain whether you are doing what you should be doing at a particular stage in your life. You must then own your situation by taking personal responsibility for where you are now and where you would like to be.

The people I coach are from all walks of life. Some are at the beginning of their working life; some are facing difficult changes mid-career, and some are reaching retirement age. However, even people in their thirties in successful careers at large multi-national companies can find themselves asking the vital question, is *this all that life is about?*

People who are happily married, but still unfulfilled in other areas of life and have lost sight of their values, may use coaching as a process to re-align their values with their goals.

People in their forties who realise they do not want to be doing the same work for the next ten years may feel the need to stop and evaluate where they are at and how they can reach their potential.

The New Generation Thinks Differently

I have seen a big change in the past twenty years. People's belief systems and actions demonstrate that setting and achieving goals have now become the norm.

While it is a slow process, change is happening. The present generation has a different mindset and I believe that little by little, the people I coach are becoming more confident and place a higher value on themselves than ever before.

Procrastination Leaves You Feeling Stuck

Generally, you find that the reason people are stuck is because they are procrastinating. This often happens when you lose sight of your values, then internally, you feel something is wrong and something is missing.

If you are procrastinating about doing something, the quickest way to move forward is by going to a coach. Coaching is great for shining a light on an area of need.

For example, if you are someone who made a promise to yourself some years back that you would lose weight but still find yourself today carrying an extra two stone around, a coach can help.

Or if you are someone who cannot drive but have been promising to learn for the longest time, coaching can also help. Or perhaps you are just stuck in a career rut and feel you cannot move forward.

It may also be the case that you have tried to do something about your situation up to now but have still been unable to move out of it. For instance, you may have tried to work through the place in which you are stuck, by talking things over with friends or family.

Coaching offers the solution here because it takes a non-judgemental, objective look at your situation. Coaching brings you into the moment where you are at now and examines how happy and fulfilled you really are.

Creating Change With Clarity And Conviction

The philosophy behind coaching is that we humans are great; that we are all on a journey of discovery to doing what we want to do. We are not on this planet just to survive, but to thrive.

While there are many reasons you get stuck in your life, by engaging with a coach who challenges you, you can return to your rightful path to reach your greater heights.

Coaching is a journey of discovery for you to acknowledge how great you are and to value the differences in others.

Coaching supports you as an individual in articulating your goals and drives you towards the desired achievement. It helps you maximise performance and produce excellent results through a supportive and challenging relationship.

The process is solution-oriented and action led. The coach empowers, supports, and challenges you with powerful questions around *what is next?* while using different tools and exercises such as neurolinguistic programming and emotional intelligence skills.

In essence coaching is about empowering you to reach your full potential. This can be done through identifying the stresses and pressures that you may be putting up with, simply for the sake of peace. It is about challenging you to be true to yourself and take appropriate action.

Sometimes people view such negative aspects of their lives as trade-offs for successes they enjoy – like having a nice home or a modern office. Even though the house may feel nothing like a home and the people they work with cause them endless stress.

Coaching is about taking personal responsibility for where you are, at a particular time and doing something about it. As the client, you have all the answers and the coach is simply there to assist in self-discovery.

The coach asks powerful questions to further self-discovery, but does not, however, provide the answers, as would a mentor. There is no hierarchy or expert role-play between you and the coach. The relationship is equal, based on the model client, coach, and the relationship. Both parties are peers, creatively and resourcefully working together towards common goals.

When coaching is complete, you will find you have developed new skills and behaviours which will translate into action and achievement. This is because the power to find the answers to your situation lies within you.

Coaching therefore is a powerful collaborative relationship between you and your coach working through a process of discovery to enable goal setting and strategic action. There is no treatment plan – the focus is on evolving and manifesting your potential.

In the coaching world I don't believe in any accidents. You are here for a reason and coaching can empower you to identify that reason.

Right now you may feel confused about where you are or where you are going, and what your life purpose is exactly. Once you re-evaluate your life with a coach, you will see yourself from a new perspective and can look objectively at where you are and face reality. This in turn helps you gain clarity on how to make progress.

In order to achieve your full potential and flourish, you must become more self-aware and create the balance that you want in your life. It is about reframing self-limiting beliefs to re-claim your power. It is about taking full control of your choices and making them happen. In doing so, you switch from doing something not because you *have to*, but because you *choose to*.

It is about looking at what change may have happened in your life and re-framing it to see this as an opportunity. An example might be, if you have lost your job, it could be about saying, *what an opportunity! I am free! I can now apply for all those jobs I have been looking at!*

By simply concentrating on just one possible change you can do to-day and taking that step, this is where the process of life coaching kicks in. Instead of blaming others for where you are right now, instead you discover that life is all about taking personal responsibility and appropriate action.

Celebrating Our Greatness

While it seems to be a cultural thing in Ireland that excelling in your life is something you are afraid to even talk about, the paradox is you all inherently want to be your best.

It all comes down to self-limiting and conditional beliefs. Unfortunately too many of you have been conditioned to think that nobody should be seen to be enjoying their life's journey. That message is also one that is often passed down from one generation to the next.

It would be such a beautiful world if you all celebrated your greatness. There would be room for each of you to excel in this world. A world where there would be no judgment, no ego, and where you would be united in togetherness rather than separation.

This would be a wonderful world!

Coaching Will Empower You

Coaching is very empowering and is a brilliant discipline to have in your life. It provides a sense of moving on and facilitates the testing out of different processes of relating, experimenting and interpreting situations from different points of view.

For people who want to improve their lives, coaching is a very valuable tool. It is the art of facilitating the performance, learning and development of another person.

A coach is your partner in helping identify where you want to go, personally and/or professionally. The coaching process is a powerful alliance designed to advance and enhance the life-long process of human learning, effectiveness, and fulfilment, which in turn develops both the coach and client.

Enjoy Personal Growth

Most people seek to enjoy personal growth throughout their lives and through coaching they can achieve progress.

Using the coaching process, for someone lacking in confidence, the client gains the confidence and self-esteem they need to speak up, even in the boardroom, if necessary. They begin to value their own opinion, and own their own choices.

Coaching Connects To What Is Inside

The reason coaching works so well is because it is brilliant at empowering you to go inside yourself to look at where your talents and skills lie. We do this by looking at what you were good at before, when you were young perhaps, enjoying something that you may have loved to do but over time were discouraged from progressing any further.

Unfortunately, in the past, our passion and creativity was not always acknowledged or encouraged as young people. In coaching I invite you to go back on your timeline to when you can remember what you loved doing during your formative years and to how good it made you feel.

For example, in my school days, I enjoyed asking questions because I was hungry for knowledge, although it was not viewed as positive. However, I believe the reason I am a brilliant coach today is because of the questions I ask my clients. I have developed the skills of being able to identify the powerful questions each client needs to ask themselves in order to advance in their lives

Coaching works because I invite you, the client, to take a helicopter view of all areas in your life. For example, I might ask you to think about how happy or fulfilled you are in each area of your life, from personal to professional. What I am looking for is your internal map of your life and how you rate it on a scale of 0 – 10.

Examining your life in this way is extremely useful because it brings attention to where you are in life and where change is needed. It can highlight some of your blind spots.

Coaching is all about empowering you to be your potential best. Leaving behind procrastination and self-limiting beliefs that may be holding you back. The process will help improve all your relationships and make you perform better at your work and in your personal life.

Life Is All About Choice

I believe that in life everyone has choices. Even children have choices but they may also have a fear that might stop them from acting on their choices.

Everything you say or do is a choice. It is like the story of two boys born into a family where their father was an alcoholic.

One is on his own and begging on the streets; the other is very successful and married.

When asked what happened, the first son says — *"What did you expect? I am just like my Dad."*

The other son says — *"My father showed me what not to do and this is why I lived my life differently and made my life a success through my freedom of choice."*

This story proves that everyone has a choice no matter what family, or situation you are born into.

This book is all about *choice*.

It is about making the choice to listen - in order to change your life.

I also believe happiness is a choice. For example, you can get up every morning and think, *'Good God it's morning'* or alternatively you can say, *'Good morning God!' This is a quote from the late Dr Wayne Dyer.*

Taking Personal Responsibility For Your Life

Once you decide to commit to coaching, you make a decision to do something serious about your situation. You take personal responsibility for your own life and engage in the process of change, so that by the end of the process, you leave with a focused plan to empower you to move forward.

In coaching the coach encourages you to turn everything negative into a positive, so that, if you are someone looking for a job, I ask that you do not view this negatively. Instead view it as a project. Tell yourself that your next project is to have a fulfilling career. The reality is you have all the resources to ensure this project becomes a reality.

If you are stuck or feeling low, reach out to a coach because a coach is someone who will never judge you. A coach will be objective and will have your best interest at heart.

Take the leap, because when you realise your dreams, you will understand that asking the questions of yourself, that you were previously afraid to ask, will have empowered you to move forward.

Coaching is absolutely powerful and it is because of attending coaching, I have made many important and profound changes in my life. Through my coaching practice, I have witnessed thousands of clients who have also made profound changes in their personal and professional life.

Through the power of coaching, I became the Personal & Executive Coach and Trainer that I am today, in the knowledge that it is my life purpose to empower people to realise they have choices and to move from *great* to *brilliant*.

I would like you to realise that you can manifest what you want in life; and that the answer to all your challenges lies within you. You can always change the perspective on how you look at things.

"If you change the way you look at things, the things you look at change." A quote from the late Dr Wayne Dyer.

This book provides a taste of what real Personal & Professional Coaching is.

A Personal & Executive Coach is focused on one thing – your success.

There is room for all of us to excel.

Your journey starts here!

Specific Life Coaching Goals

Coaching is about maximising performance and becoming the best you can be – a natural ambition that each of us seek to fulfil.

Breaking it down on a step-by-step basis, life coaching can empower you to achieve a whole range of goals, listed on the next page.

Life coaching can empower you:

- *Change career*
- *Move out of a bad relationship*
- *Take full responsibility for your life*
- *Have the lifestyle you want*
- *Achieve a healthy weight and lifestyle*
- *Have fun in your life and take up new activities*
- *Move away from friends that drain you and surround yourself with like-minded people*
- *Raise your level of consciousness*
- *Move to the next level of expansion in your life to reach your full potential*
- *Move house, move country*
- *When faced with too many choices make the right choice*
- *Identify your strengths and weaknesses*
- *Get the job you want/ Leave a job you hate*
- *Do things you never thought possible*
- *Look at things differently and think outside the box*
- *Be true to yourself and your values and live a life of peace and integrity*
- *Value your time*
- *Be assertive and stand up for yourself at work*
- *Gain confidence and believe in yourself*
- *Identify goals and what is important when you have lost sight of your values*
- *Speak up and be heard*
- *Find the person you want to be with*
- *Create space in your life for happiness*
- *Live a work/life balance*
- *Open a window of opportunity*
- *Rise above a challenge by seeing it as an opportunity*
- *Open your own business*
- *Not to settle for "less than" in a job or relationship*
- *Be true to yourself and move to take full responsibility in your life*
- *Stop procrastinating and break bad habits*
- *Be open, honest, and loving*
- *Become more understanding, caring, and patient*
- *Become more willing to listen to others and their perspectives*

- *Stop being your own strongest critic*
- *Be more loving and caring towards yourself and then in turn, others*
- *Understand rather than need to be understood*
- *Move away from being judgemental*
- *Help you become the best you can be*

This Book Will Empower You To Move On

In these pages, I share a number of anonymous but real-life case studies and practical exercises that will provide you with a clearer picture of how you can map out your own life in order to manifest your goals and dreams.

These case studies link into each other in such a way as to cover different aspects of your personality or life habits that may be working against you.

They include career, relationship and personal growth stories and exercises which will help you view your own life from a fresh perspective and identify possible blockages in your path.

I would like you to realise you have a choice in life. Asking yourself some of the life coaching questions I share with you in this book and answering them truthfully will create for you a positive mindset change and take actions which will lead to positive results in your life.

These new actions will create for you a new perspective on your world. Even looking at just one aspect of your life in a more curious way can help make a difference.

If you are a person for whom the opinion of others matters to the point where what they believe appears more important than what you think, be true to yourself and begin to honour and value your own opinion.

Realise the only person who can get you out of your problematic situation is you. You choose what you believe in and once you take personal responsibility for your life, you will move on.

Once you complete the coaching exercises honestly and comprehensively you will find you can turn the corner to be able to do what you want to do.

By developing my skills as a Personal & Executive Coach, I have seen so many people, un-tap their own true potential and I have also seen people give up on life too easily simply because they have failed to appreciate that life is truly precious.

Sometimes I see the potential in people before they acknowledge it in themselves. By by-passing your ego, you reach into your own heart and grow as a person.

I believe that in life we all need mentors or coaches. I was mentored as a young owner of a restaurant. My mentor really believed in me and coached me to run the restaurant to a high level of success.

Life Gets Better The Day You Are Ready To Listen

People understand the importance of listening when it applies to their physical body.

For example, a client might tell me something that happened in their life and remark: *"My body was telling me this but I didn't listen."*

Or: *"My friends told me this but I didn't want to hear it."*

When I am coaching clients on how they can choose to listen to the messages that are there for them, they often experience *light bulb moments.*

A client might say – *"My Dad always told me I was good at this but I just wasn't ready to listen."*

The day you are ready to listen – to both the internal intuitive messages as well as the external messages - that's the day your life will change for the better.

When you are in what is called *"the flow"*, which means you are on purpose and doing the work you love, you are listening to your intuition and the messages that are there for you.

When you go against your value system, you cannot listen to the messages and intuitively you know this, because you feel uneasy.

The process is about tuning in and becoming acutely self-aware.

Self-awareness is being aware of what is happening inside of you right now; why you are feeling this way.

It is about becoming your own observer of how you are feeling at a given time.

Making the effort to stop and think about how you are feeling helps you become more aware of why you say *yes* or *no* to particular situations or people.

This in turn highlights your value system and in order to be in tune with your value system, you need to listen to the messages coming from your mind and body.

Two

· ·

The Factors That Influence Your Personality

Your Belief System

Your beliefs are what drive you. They are intangible and frequently unconscious. They are often confused with facts. A fact is usually something that has happened, whereas a belief is a generalisation about what will happen. It is a guiding principle. Some of our beliefs give us freedom, choice, and open possibilities.

Beliefs are formed haphazardly throughout our life from the meaning we give to our experience.

In my 23 years of experience as a coach, I believe that beliefs and values exert such a powerful influence over your life, they amount to one of the most important areas in coaching to be worked on with a client.

The fact is you are the product of your belief system and your beliefs are the product of who you are and your value system. In other words you become your belief system.

Although your beliefs can give you freedom, choice and open possibilities, other beliefs may disempower you, affect your behaviour in a negative way and close down your choices.

Other beliefs disempower us by shutting us down and controlling our behaviour, which in turn closes off our choices.

"Whether you think you can, or you think you can't, you're right". – A quote from Henry Ford.

Some of our beliefs come from our past experiences.

I often ask my clients – *Are you living now based on your past experiences?*

In other words, are you stuck in the *now* because of your past experiences and beliefs about that experience?

It is not possible to quantify how many beliefs you have, because from one experience to the next you automatically form beliefs.

Often our beliefs are totally self-constructed. Others can be conditional beliefs handed down traditionally from generation to generation.

Where you believe you should not anticipate a good outcome or success in what you are trying to do, based on the advice *"not to count your chickens before they hatch"* - this is a conditional belief, not a fact.

Similarly, when clients in coaching tell me they believe that Irish people have a habit of being late, I refute this statement because it is simply not true – it is a false belief.

When you were born into this world, you had no beliefs, but very quickly you formed initial primary impressions from your parents, then perhaps from the crèche, your school, teachers, friends, family, college and work. As you moved on, you formed beliefs from your experiences in life.

How parents communicate with their children plays a central role in how beliefs are formed. When parents make mistakes they should set the example, that it is normal to make mistakes. It is part of life to make mistakes and to always learn the lessons from the experience. Such example of learning will formulate a good belief and value system for a child.

As stated, some of your beliefs are formed by your experiences. If you have had a bad relationship experience you might attach a meaning to this that all relationships end badly, but of course this is not true. There are wonderful people out there. It is just that you are basing your beliefs on past experiences.

Beliefs can be formed as a result of unexpected conflict, traumas and confusion. The younger you are when such events occur, the more likely such false beliefs are likely to form. While some choose to explain where they are now because of their past, the key is to refuse to dwell on the past. It is what you do with what happens to you in your life that matters. If you evaluate and take the learning from that experience, you can move forward with a positive message that you are doing great now. Everything is ok.

You can either spend your time in the '*land of lack*' or the '*land of abundance*'. You have a choice in every single thing you do and say. Gratitude and acceptance is positive. Complaining and resentment is negative.

If you remain annoyed and angry at mistakes of the past you will stay stuck because anger will keeps you stuck. Losing sight of your values and what is important to you will mean you lose sight of who you are.

It comes down to acknowledging the past, respecting it and moving on. Then you are in a position to appreciate and value what you have today. While you might never get the same opportunities again, it is about viewing things differently by looking at what you do with what you have now.

From past experiences you learn not to make the same mistakes again, while through re-examining your values and needs, you come to know what you want and really value in life.

Your belief system is very important as it formulates your value system in terms of what is important to you in your life.

Self-Limiting Beliefs

Unfortunately, it is human nature to maximise the negative which means you always give thought to bad things people say to you and allow them to form in your consciousness as negative self-limiting beliefs. Self-limiting beliefs take your power away and can control and even destroy your life. It stops you from being the best version of who you are.

Acting out on these beliefs as if they were true, makes you and others around you miserable. For example, when you speak in terms of *'I can't'*; *'I shouldn't'*; *'I suppose'* or use other passive terms such as: *'maybe'*; *'let's see how it goes/play it by ear'*; *'I might'*; *'I'll try'*- you either do or you don't! To try is an in-action word with no results. Using these terms are excuses because they are non-committal.

Other self-limiting beliefs can be as a result of fear of success, which then acts to hold you back from many jobs and other life opportunities. This fear could be defined as believing that you really *'can't have your cake and eat it'*.

You do not deliberately choose to have self-limiting beliefs but they come up again and again from past references and experiences. Sometimes you may harbour these self-limiting beliefs as a result of things people you admire may have said to you in the past. For example, someone you saw as a role model, said something negative to you. You may tend to take them at their word, even if they are wrong in what they said.

Typical self-limiting beliefs are:

'I'm not good enough'; *'Nobody believes in me'*; *'I'm not important'*.

The *'I'm not good enough'* self-limiting belief is a very common problem for lots of people and comes from trying to live life to the standard of you, as a perfectionist, or to somebody else's standard.

Of course, you can never be happy if you live your life under this pressure because you are constantly thinking, *'I have to do this'* or *'I have to do that'* in relation to everything you do. You constantly compare yourself to others and continue the self-limiting belief – *"I'm not good enough"*.

'I can't do something' is also a self-limiting belief, because when you say it, you close down every possibility of doing anything positive.

Similarly thinking, *'I don't have enough, I'm not educated enough, who do I think I am, I am afraid, I am fearful'*- these are all examples of self-limiting beliefs that take your power away.

Telling yourself *'Nobody else can do this but me'* – for example at work. This is also a self-limiting belief, coming from your ego. This results in you not delegating and taking on too much work.

When you take on personal responsibility and realise you do not have to do everything as you have a choice, you then become empowered about how you choose to live your life.

Removing Self-Limiting Beliefs

When a client comes to coaching a decision has been made by the client to make positive changes and commit to the process of achieving new goals.

In the process of coaching, I elicit from the client their self-limiting beliefs. We work together to replace those self-limiting beliefs with new positive beliefs and affirmations. It is imperative that these affirmations resonate and fit in with the client's core values and sense of self.

Clearing all self-limiting beliefs is necessary to achieve the successful fulfilled life the client desires. It is easy to make this change, once the client has given permission to do so. I like to use the phrase *'Catch them, challenge them and clear them.'*

You can begin by removing *"if"* and replacing the word with *"when"*. *"If"* introduces doubt which prevents you from achieving your best.

Also tell yourself when clearing self-limiting beliefs:

'From today I am not giving any more energy to this self-limiting belief.

In coaching, I invite you to feel and imagine how holding onto a self-limiting belief has served you to date. Once you find that this self-limiting belief is only serving you in a negative way, you will readily let go of this self-limiting belief and work to replace this self-limiting belief with a positive affirmation.

It takes 27- 30 days of regularly repeating an affirmation and feeling it fully, to remove a self-limiting belief. Once you form the affirmations to counter your self-limiting beliefs you will find that after this time the self-limiting beliefs will fade away. Generally, in my coaching practice I do not work with clients to use affirmations to manifest, but to clear out self-limiting beliefs to make room for manifesting.

For example, I worked with a client who reported that her car had been clamped and this was typical, because she believed she was just *'unlucky.'* She had also recently lost her purse and believed it had been stolen from her and there were no good and honest people.

She had a self-limiting belief around the idea that she was "unlucky." I worked with her on changing that self-limiting belief. She believed that some people were born lucky and this did not include her.

The same client later received a call to tell her that her purse and all the money in it had been found. She was very happy to receive this news, and more importantly the realisation that there are good and honest people in the world and it is not about luck.

This shows that the power lies within us to decide what to focus on. In this client's case, she was upset about her car being clamped, and feeling unlucky. When she discovered someone had picked up her purse and had taken the trouble to return it to her, a paradigm shift occurred, and she eliminated from her life her two self-limiting beliefs around luck and people and formed a new affirmation/statement.

The client's new Affirmation was – "I believe there are good and honest people in the world and I create my own luck."

Affirmations

Affirmations, which are statements or declarations to yourself that something is true, are very positive in helping to change self-limiting beliefs and behaviour patterns.

Some examples of affirmations are as follows:

'I only attract like-minded people into my life every day.'

'I believe I am a loving and powerful person and people are attracted to me because I care about them.'

An affirmation cannot be a lie and it must reflect your values. By believing you are a powerful and caring person you can attract people into your life who have the same values.

Affirmations around work could be:

'Today is going to be a very productive day'.

'I believe people listen to me with enthusiasm and respect.'

Saying this latter affirmation frees you up from having to worry about what other people think of you. This enables you to be your true self at all times.

Affirmations around relationships could be:

I am attracting a like-minded, loving person into my life right now.

Exercise

Creating affirmations around self-limiting beliefs

To form an affirmation, go to the self-limiting belief and reframe the belief as a positive affirmation.	*Refer to the examples to help you get started.*

The affirmation should focus on relying on your own personal resources to achieve a desired outcome.

Never use the words *'I deserve'* in an affirmation as this refers to the ego.

The affirmations must be stated in the present tense; they must be positive and personal (for example, *'I value my time and choose how I spend it'*).

To identify what self-limiting beliefs exist in your life and what new affirmations/beliefs are required to replace them, ask yourself the following questions:

How is this current self-limiting belief serving me?

How will my life be better with this new belief I am creating?

How might it be worse?

What is the best thing that can happen if I keep my old self-limiting belief?

What is the best thing that can happen if I move to my new belief?

Other Examples Of Affirmations

I have all the resources within me to manage this situation

Money flows easily and effortlessly to me every day

I have the resources to find the money to fulfil my true potential in life

My fulfilling career is on its way to me right now

I can achieve anything I choose to achieve

I only focus on what I can do something about

Add your own affirmations to the list
_____

(Jot them down on the space below)
_____

How One Word Has A Different Meaning For Two People

Example

Imagine there are two people talking about what divorce means to them.

The first person is so horrified that divorce has entered his life. He describes "Divorce" as the most ugly and painful word in the English vocabulary. He married and loved his wife. He believed that they were two people brought together in love, and was shocked to learn that his wife wanted to divorce him. He felt powerless in the process and felt he had no choice. He is now divorced and hates having to accept a status in life that he never thought would apply to him.

The second person who has also gone through a divorce, views the word in a completely contrasting way. This person, says that "Divorce" is the best thing that has ever happened to her. She felt she had been living in a prison and being divorced gave her a sense of freedom. The best thing she ever did, was to initiate proceedings and go through with the divorce.

The Importance Of Positive Empowering Beliefs

You need to know and believe in who you are. Therefore it is very important to have positive beliefs about who you are, the world and the people you come into contact with.

Some people allow what happened in their past to affect how they behave in the present and this means they are not living fully in the present. Instead they are living from a false belief system.

Often just one negative remark or comment designed to criticise, can drain your energy and vitality. However, when you have a positive belief system it need not have any impact.

Once you have a positive belief system you are in control, so that no matter what happens, you can remind yourself you have a choice to make about what is happening and how you are going to move on from it.

Having a positive belief system can be achieved deliberately through filling your world with positive affirmations and always choosing what to focus on.

If a self-limiting belief comes into your mind, the best approach is to allow yourself to wallow in misery for a couple of minutes, and then immediately move your focus to what you can do about the situation and form an affirmation. It is all about moving on. You are focusing on bringing power back to yourself.

Exercise

Making a list of Empowering Beliefs

Having a very empowering belief that 'no matter what happens I can handle it' is a quote from Susan Jeffers — "Feel the Fear and do it anyway".

There are thousands of empowering beliefs, which can be as basic as telling yourself:

'I believe I am a friendly, positive, powerful, intelligent person';

'I believe I am a good person';

'I believe I am a beautiful person';

'I can do anything I want';

'I can achieve anything I want to achieve'.

'I believe I have a positive outlook on life.'

'I believe I am a good communicator.'

'I believe I have integrity/honesty.'

'I believe I have inner strength.'

'I believe I am a good husband/wife/father/mother/son/daughter/friend.'

'I am a kind/good person.'

'I have the skills I need to achieve my goals.'

'I give 100% to any task I undertake.'

'I believe I am a good motivational leader.'

'I believe I am people oriented.'

'I believe I am a good listener.'

'I believe I am a good person.'

The most empowering belief you can ever have is:

'I choose.'

This brings with it the power of choice and once you believe you can choose your situation and what you do or say, you are back in your own power. You can claim whatever problem or mistake arises, name it then return to your power to deal with it and move on.

Take some time to write a list of empowering beliefs that can help you in your life.	*Refer to the examples above to help you get started.*

Tips

After saying affirmations that resonate with you for *30 days in succession*, the new belief system takes over from the old belief system as mentioned in work from *"Brian Tracy"*.

Naturally there will be a shift of energy and people will notice this. There will also be a shift in your nervous system as you adjust to the new you.

The best approach is to say the affirmations as often as possible throughout the day, perhaps associating them with certain activities.

Alternatively you could save your affirmations in written/typed form so that they appear as background on your phone or computer.

Say your affirmations/positive statements first thing in the morning, last thing at night and as frequently as you can throughout the day.

You need to say your affirmations regularly throughout the day for them to sink in and resonate and cause change in you.

This is not about false thinking i.e. sowing weeds and telling yourself you are sowing flowers. You are not lying to yourself.

Affirmations work because you say them with energy and conviction and then you bring this energy in to your life for real.

Ideally, display your affirmations in as many places as possible where you can readily see them, to remind you of the new belief system you want to create.

You can also reinforce these new empowering beliefs by visualising and anticipating the benefits the new belief will yield for you.

If you happen to miss a day of saying your affirmations, start the process again, for a full 27 - 30 days again.

You need to say them each day in succession as this is how long it takes for a change in your belief system to take place.

Values And The Importance Of Knowing Your Value System

Your beliefs are what drive you and they formulate your value system.

It is very important to remember that behind every result lies your decision and behind every decision lies your value system and behind your value system lies your beliefs.

There are three types of values.

We have Global values, which are what most of us want in the world, such as peace and harmony. However, in coaching we work on Core Values and Personal Values.

Core Values are the most important people or things that you wish to spend time on in your life. In order to determine your core values you need to think deeply about what is important to you.

Personal Values, can be integrity, honesty, and ambition. These are values that you possess within yourself. In order to meet a like-minded person, whether as a friend or as a significant other, you must know your own personal values and seek to discover theses values in the other person.

You may not be consciously aware of your values, yet if someone asks you to do something and you feel uneasy inside, you recognise that this feeling is because you are going against your values.

For example, if someone asks you to lie for them and you immediately feel discomfort, this is because it goes against your values of honesty and integrity.

Your personal values tell you who you are in life, and the fastest route to knowing yourself, is to identify these values.

Tip

To live a life of integrity and freedom, I encourage you to do an internal check on every decision you make. Ask yourself what are you saying "yes" to, and what are you saying "no" to, making sure you stay in alignment with your values.

Doing so, will give you peace of mind and freedom because instinctively when you go against your value system, you immediately get a feeling that something is wrong.

Core Values

Our Core Values are the most important people or things in life that we wish to spend time on. Examples of Core Values are, family, home, health, career and hobbies.

These values are what you want to work on, and commit to, in order to achieve your goals.

At any one time, you take action on your top 5 core values. As you develop as a person, you naturally change your core value system in order of importance.

For example, when you are young, travel may be very important as one of your top 5 core values.

However, when you decide to make a career change of your choice, your core value of career might move up in its order of importance in your top 5 core values.

Similarly, for someone who does not have someone special in their life, they might make it a core value to meet a significant other.

Therefore core values are unique to everybody.

If something, or someone is a core value in your life you will already be acting on it, because core values drive every action you take.

If there is an area you are not working on, or focused on, it is because you do not have it in your top five core values.

If you choose to ignore your core values, you are more likely to feel internal tension and frustration.

The price of not being true to your own core values is a sense of selling out on yourself, resulting in an unfulfilling life, that is propped up by having to choose to tolerate and settle for "less than", rather than a life of "fulfilment".

For example, if you are saying *"yes"* to everything to do with work, you may be choosing to say *"no"* to time with family or friends. Everything is about choice. You choose to let your core values rise or drop in priority.

You can never force your values on anybody else.

Example, if there is something you observe another person doing that you may not morally agree with, it is not for you to judge the person living their life in this way. You must accept that it is "their value" to behave in this way.

You need to know what is important to you in life, because if you do not know what is important, how will you get to where you want to go?

You will simply move aimlessly about, drifting along, without challenging yourself to achieve anything at all.

We all have expectations, targets and goals and behind all of these are your core values.

By clarifying your core values you can create a map that will guide you in making the decisions you need to make in order to advance in life.

You will discover what is truly essential to you and this will help you take a stand and make choices based on what is fulfilling to you.

Exercise

Identifying your core values

In order to identify your core values ask yourself the following:

1. *What do I want to spend most of my time on in my life?*

Write your answers in the form of a list and rate them number 1–10. Your top five values will be numbers 1–5.

Another powerful question to consider is:

2. *Who do I want to spend most of my time with?*

3. *What is my dream career?*

4. *If I was to leave the world tomorrow, who would be the people I would like to bring with me and what things would I like to take?*

Tip

Make sure to give priority to your most important core values.

Everything that is a choice raises your energy – you choose to do it.

Once you have taken action on an area of your life – you are allowing it to become a core value. You can then set goals in alignment with your core values.

Personal Values

Personal values relate to what characteristics you value in yourself and others.

Examples here could be integrity, generosity, kindness, supportiveness etc.

One of the reasons people don't know their value system is because they don't consciously focus on their values or bring attention to them.

They simply never think about their value system.

Values And Relationships

In relationships, values play a big part. It must not be ignored, that quite often opposite temperaments can attract like a magnet.

You may know of somebody who is predominately very visual, (they experience life through their visual filter), attracted like a magnet to somebody who is predominately very auditory, (they experience life through their detailed filter). Fifteen months later however, the strain may start to show when one person realises that while they like the world of the opposite temperament in their partner, they don't want the same things in life; and so it all comes back to values.

Alternatively you can have someone who settles for a partner who shares the same temperament and sees things in the same way. These couples can often stay together because it is safe but if you see them out in a restaurant together you may notice they are not talking.

This is because they are probably bored out of their minds with each other, but decide to stick together because security is one of their top core values.

Generally, the best relationship is where partners have opposite temperaments, however share the same value system.

Therefore, they want the same things in life and want to enjoy the same experiences and their differing temperaments, will keep the journey together interesting and challenging.

If you can't identify what personal values you want in someone else, this means you don't know what your own personal values are to begin with. Therefore the first step must always be to know your own personal and core values at all times.

How To Identify Another Person's Values?

When you meet someone for the first time, you can identify what some of their values are.

For example, it is easy to identify that a person values fashion by the clothes they wear. It can also be easy to discover if they value communication by the way they interact with people and also by their body language and demeanour.

Some people are very strong in outwardly expressing their values while others are not.

For example, you can tell the moment a person walks in to a room if they value attention and being listened to or whether they value their own space by sitting away from people at the back of the room, so they are not being seen or drawing attention to themselves.

What other people pay attention to, can demonstrate their values.

For example, if someone spends a lot of time talking about politics, the value at play here could be the need for a voice of freedom and/or having their opinion as a person valued.

You must go behind the platform to see what value is inspiring this person, because the value defines purpose and meaning.

Alternatively people can lie to themselves about what their values really are, for instance in matters of the heart.

Someone may claim to be open to meeting someone new to share their life with. However, when an opportunity arises to go on a date, they may make an excuse and refuse.

This is because sometimes people just lie to themselves.

Living A Life In Alignment With Your Core And Personal Values

Most of the time it is possible to live in accordance with our core and personal values but we are also human and therefore likely to make mistakes.

For those who succeed in living in alignment with their values there is a great feeling of peace, integrity, and freedom in their lives. They mean what they say and they walk their own talk.

Conversely, when you go against your value system, there is a feeling of internal failure. This goes deeper and is more harming to you because other people don't know about it, only you know about it and therefore only you can do something about it.

There could be a situation where in your life you are settling "for less than", by staying in a relationship you don't want to be in, simply because you value the financial situation higher than being in love. Placing a higher value on finance and security over love and happiness makes it impossible for you to leave this relationship.

However, knowing that you put these values ahead of your own happiness will eat away at you with the result that over time, you may get very sick and even depressed if you fail to make a change.

Sadly for some people, their reality is that security is their highest value. They will not leave their relationship and risk losing this security no matter how unhappy they may become. In this instance, they move towards security as their highest value and move away from love and happiness.

Consequently, they know they are just settling "for less than" rather than seeking to thrive and realise their full happiness and potential as a person.

Exercise

Clarification Of Personal Values

The most effective way to clarify personal values is to extract them from your own experience.

In order to do this, draw up a list of your personal values as they are now.

Use the list provided as a guide to choose your personal values and jot them down below.

Once you have identified your top 10 values rank them in order from highest to lowest and then rate yourself on how well you are honouring your values on a scale of 1 to 10.

This exercise will help you both to identify your personal values and also reveal how true you are being to your authentic self.

Use the space below to list your personal values.

Benevolence	Bliss	Boldness
Bravery	Brilliance	Calmness
Candour	Capability	Care
Control	Conviction	Courage
Courtesy	Creativity	Credibility
Curiosity	Daring	Decisiveness
Deference	Delight	Dependability
Depth	Desire	Determination
Devotion	Devoutness	Dignity
Diligence	Direction	Directness
Discipline	Discovery	Discretion
Diversity	Flexibility	Flow
Fluency	Focus	Fortitude
Frankness	Freedom	Friendliness
Frugality	Fun	Generosity
Giving	Grace	Gratitude
Gregariousness	Growth	Guidance
Happiness	Harmony	Health
Heart	Helpfulness	Holiness
Honesty	Honour	Hopefulness
Hospitality	Humility	Humour
Hygiene	Imagination	Impact
Impartiality	Independence	Inquisitiveness
Inspiration	Integrity	Intelligence
Intensity	Intimacy	Intuition
Justice	Keenness	Kindness
Knowledge	Leadership	Learning
Liberty	Liveliness	Logic
Love	Loyalty	Making a difference
Mastery	Maturity	Mellowness
Meticulousness	Mindfulness	Modesty
Motivation	Mysteriousness	Neatness
Nerve	Obedience	Open-mindedness
Openness	Optimism	Order
Originality	Power	Passion

Four

· ·

Manifesting And Creating
The Life You Desire

Manifestation is a way of attracting into your life what you desire.

It is one of the most powerful tools available to help you achieve the life of your dreams.

It describes the process whereby you focus your mind on a particular goal in order to make it a reality.

This focus could be a car, a house or a desire to even meet a new person in your life.

Whatever we focus on we can manifest.

Whatever the mind believes and conceives – it is already achieved.

You just need to go into the process and get what it is you desire.

It will be there waiting for you in the Universe.

Manifestation is an art and a discipline that is accessible to all and offers a wonderful way of creating the life you desire.

It helps you get what you want in life simply by focusing on it.

It is about working from your true self.

It relates to your belief system and what you believe – and also relates to how self-aware you are.

Manifesting is working with our internal self, projecting onto life what we want to attract in and believing that we can do it.

It is coming from within us.

If you believe, without any doubt in your mind, that you can achieve something or attract something into your life; and if you can actually visualise what you want as though it is already there in your life – followed by an affirmation with feeling - then there is a 99% chance you will achieve it.

Manifesting comes about as a result of belief with no doubt and an absolute trust that you are connected to the universe.

Some people chose not to acknowledge the power of manifesting because they have different beliefs and mindsets.

Negative Manifesting

Manifesting can equally work to create negativity in your life if, instead of focusing on positive influences and desires, you are someone who dwells on what is wrong in your life.

By concentrating on what is wrong in your life, you attract more negativity into your life, because whatever you focus on you expand in your life.

This is why it is so important to become self-aware and particularly aware of what you think and focus on.

Manifesting Your Potential

To excel at life – in what you do and the life you lead - you must go to the end result and work backwards.

What this means is you must set a vision for what you want in your life and invest time and energy into thinking about it and taking steps to make it happen.

You must name your vision in the present tense and then go into detail on how you are going to achieve it.

It is a matter of writing it down and attracting it in.

Your vision should involve your senses as much as possible so that you can see, feel, touch and observe yourself in action living the life you desire.

In order to start the process, you must choose to take action.

This can be in the form of baby steps, where you make a phone call or turn up at an event relevant to something or someone you want to attract into your life.

Nothing can happen without you taking action.

This means you must put yourself out there meeting people. The people you want to connect with are not just going to turn up and knock on your door.

Your heart must be open to whatever happens.

Once you set the wheels in motion it can happen quicker than you realise.

Energy And Manifesting

Everybody can manifest!!

Once you are awakened to the fact that as vibrational beings all of us are connected to each other through energy, you can make manifestations happen.

In my own life, I have a friend who always texts me when I am feeling a little depressed. I only think of her and she rings me. This connection is so strong, it is because we are all connected and particularly to people who share our values and with whom we have a lot in common.

The important thing is to be open to everything and closed to nothing, in order for things to happen.

Manifesting is all about energy. We are energy beings on this earth having a human experience.

When you walk into a social event or any space where there are people, you can immediately detect energy vibrations and whether they are good or bad.

All of us do this, whether we are aware of it or not. We sense the energy.

If something serious has just been said or the atmosphere is tense, we feel it.

It is like we are connected to different channels of our existence.

In order to manifest you need to be in a place of high energy, so that you can say your affirmations and believe them.

When your energy is high you manifest far quicker.

If you are at a low energy level when you say your daily affirmations, where your emotions are being ruled by shame or perhaps guilt, you will never manifest successfully.

This is because negative emotions impact your reality and this is why it is important to calibrate body energy.

Powerful Word Changes Can Generate High Energy

If you are thinking about what you have achieved you are in a place of high energy, which enables you to manifest and achieve more very quickly.

If your energy is low however, the only way to bring it high again is to change the words in your thoughts.

For example, if you are thinking about your work in terms of how tired it makes you feel and how much you dislike it, you could choose to shift your thinking in the following way:

'I choose to do this work because it facilitates my long-term goal''.

Similarly, someone who thinks totally negatively about their life might tell themselves:

'Nothing ever works out for me.'

This person needs to form an affirmation/statement to counteract this negative statement. For example:

'Everything I choose to do I achieve with excellent results.'

As with all affirmations, this person must decide to take on the new positive statement by saying it for 27- 30 days in order to cast their self-limiting beliefs aside.

Generally, by day 27–30 they will have undergone a paradigm shift that will alter their mindset to a positive one.

Test Your Client

Often, I do the *muscle test* on clients and this is a simple aid to help detect energy levels.

The body never lies.

The test begins when I ask my client to name one task that they feel they "have to" do by the end of the week. They don't enjoy it, however they must complete it.

I request my client to hold out their arm and say the words out loud while they try to resist me by pressing up, as I press down on their arm.

'I have to do my taxes by the end of the week.'

As my client said these words and I pressed on her arm, her arm sank down completely.

Next, I invited my client to change just one word in the sentence, by saying:

'I choose to do my taxes by the end of the week.'

As my client spoke these words, I again pressed down on her arm, but this time her arm resisted and stayed up.

After completing this exercise, I asked my client how she felt about tackling the task and she replied that she felt good and very energised about completing the task.

There is one simple explanation for this result. When you feel and believe I *"have to"* do this, someone or something is controlling your life. You are accountable to another person, situation or the world. This leaves the client in a state of feeling *out of control,* which is the statement that describes stress.

So when you change the words from *"having to"*, to *"choosing to"* it immediately brings you back into your power in a very positive and energetic way. You are now in charge of your life.

Exercise

Changing Your Words To Reduce Your Resistance With The Help Of A Colleague

The muscle test shows very clearly how every word we use affects our emotions.

Complete this simple exercise on yourself, with the help of a colleague, as follows:

Articulate out loud a task you must complete but that you do not feel happy about.

Now change the wording so that you say you 'choose' to do the task.

Articulate the new wording out loud several times, placing emphasis where you say 'I choose'.

Feel your resistance ebb away.

Paradigm Shift

Where a change from negative to positive is needed you are told a paradigm shift needs to take place.

People sometimes become confused about what this means and whether they can achieve such a shift, but actually we go through paradigm shifts in our lives every day.

It happens when we tap into our inner resources to shift from one level of performance to another.

What is happening in effect is, we are changing from one behavioural mode to another.

For example, consider you have just had an argument with someone and within a short time, you arrive at your workplace to be greeted by a client at the door. Immediately you switch from your emotional mode of anger to a calm and professional mode to greet and welcome the client, leaving the argument completely behind you.

Many similar examples of 'paradigm shifts' can take place during a person's day which shows we are all moving through paradigm shifts on an ongoing basis without even knowing it.

What happens is, a change of mindset takes place that allows you to move from one frame of mind to another.

Manifesting Day To Day

In my own life I have so many personal stories that have come about through manifestation. I lived in the house I manifested 19 years ago.

My friends call me the Queen of Manifestation and I would recommend its practice to everyone. Once you become proficient at manifesting, everything falls into place.

Generally I use affirmations to manifest. When my energy is low, I make sure to say them every morning. By the time I get through my list of affirmations I feel very positive.

"I only focus on what I can do something about", is one of my favourite affirmations.

The process is all about saying your affirmations with energy, letting it go and believing it can happen.

For my goals to be realised, I need to be at a high energy level in my body to manifest. I also add to all my affirmations for manifesting – *"for my higher good and the higher good of all"*.

I focus on maintaining this high energy state and I no longer have any self- limiting beliefs. I therefore use my affirmations directly to manifest.

Examples Of Manifestations

Manifestation Of My Home

The manifestation of my home arose at a time when I had four months to sort out a new living situation. I put together a vision board of what I wanted the house to look and be like.

On the vision board, I described the house of my dreams: very low maintenance, with wooden or tiled floors.

I also described a small garden at the back of the house, and for no particular reason other than I was always drawn to the area, I started an affirmation as follows:

'I am now living in my 3- bedroom house in my ideal location.'

Four months later I was living there.

I said this affirmation every day, about 10 times throughout the day.

A few days later, I was at the bank and met an ex-student I hadn't seen for some time. We arranged to meet for a catch-up over coffee. She knew nothing about my situation and I was not aware that her mother had passed away since we last spoke.

During our conversation, I shared with her that I was *looking for a house in my ideal location.*

She shared with me –

'You will not believe this; my dad is about to put up a sign for an agent to sell the house. The house is in your ideal location.'

I asked if I could see the house as soon as possible.

I went out to see the house and fell in love with it immediately.

In my studies on manifesting, I had read that you must own what you want to manifest, you must mark it as yours.

I took an earring out of my ear and put it in a space between the kitchen cabinet tiles. I said to my friend:

'I will be back to take that earring out.'

With that I knew the process had started.

I sought loan approval for a mortgage, despite my accountant telling me I would not be approved for the loan I needed.

I told the accountant that the house was mine. I went for a meeting with the bank and was informed that they would issue their decision regarding my loan application the following week.

Meanwhile a *Mind, Body and Spirit* show was taking place in Dublin and I went along to see what was happening.

I was invited to enter a free competition by writing my name and address.

I decided to write my new address in my ideal location, because in my mind I was going to be living in this house.

Five days later my ex-student rang and said:

'There is post here for you at this address'

I told her there was no loan approval yet, but assured her the money was on its way and that I decided that this house was my home.

Two weeks later I received approval for the loan and moved into my house.

Manifestation Of A Prize

One morning I was at a business network meeting and felt very connected to the speaker. She said, *'I have a lovely gift of CD's of Deepak Chopra for one of you here to win today.'*

I looked at the prize and because I am a fan of Deepak Chopra I decided that these CDs were mine. More than 40 names were going into a hat from which a winner would be drawn.

When the draw took place, my name was pulled out of the hat and I won the prize.

In order to manifest these CD's into my reality, during the speaker's presentation I repeated over and over to myself,

'The CDs are for me; they are meant for me; they're coming my way.'

And so they did!

Manifestation Of Winning Tickets

My young son wanted to go to a particular kiddies' event, but tickets were all sold out. I did not want him to be disappointed and so every morning I assured him we are going to the Santa Fair!

On a radio station one day I heard a presenter announce he had two tickets to give away for the event. In order to win, I had to send in the reason my child should win the tickets.

As I was in the car I decided to visualise my entry being sent off for the competition. I visualised the letter I would write and saw it arrive at the radio station and being selected as the winning entry.

I sent my entry.

Approximately three weeks later I received a phone call on my mobile and a woman asked had I entered the Santa Fair competition.

When I confirmed I had, she declared that my son and I were the chosen winners.

She sent out the tickets and we both went on to enjoy a wonderful day!

Manifestation Of Important Personal Papers

On one occasion, I lost some very important personal papers. However, when I discovered the loss, instead of panicking I decided to manifest and say the following affirmation/statement:

'Some good person out there is going to pick up my papers and send them back to me.'

It would have cost me thousands Euros to redo all of the work contained in those personal papers and so I repeatedly told myself on a daily basis that my papers would be found and returned to me.

A few weeks later a brown envelope with my name on it arrived at my house. Inside a note read:

'My son found these papers on the street. We opened up the folder because it looked serious. That is how we found your name and address. We thought you might need these papers and so decided to send them back to you."

My personal work was sent home to me safely exactly as I believed it would be, because there are good people in this world.

Manifestation Of The Perfect Car

Once on a coaching course I was presenting, a girl shared a story about manifesting a particular car into her life, which sounded quite unbelievable to others in the room.

However I find it easy to believe such stories, because I know from personal experience you can visualise what you want and it will turn up.

The girl stated that she had really wanted a red car with white leather seats – which was a very specific and an unusual request.

She said she had been reading about the law of attraction and in order to make her wish a reality, had started saying the following affirmation every day:

I am now driving my red car with white leather seats.

Her mother told her not to be so ridiculous, that she could never attract a car like that with the income she was earning. However the girl kept saying her affirmation and kept believing that the car would manifest into her life.

In the meantime, she met a wealthy guy and after some time they became engaged. Her engagement present from her Fiancé, was a red car with white leather seats.

She had never shared her affirmation for such a car with him. She simply manifested it into her life!

Manifesting My Ideal Office Partner

In November 2015 I started to say an Affirmation – "I am now attracting my ideal partner to share my office with". I said this Affirmation three or four times daily.

In February 2016, a lady who had completed my Accredited Diploma six years ago called me to discuss some coaching Sessions around her Career.

Coming towards the end of the fourth session, the lady through the work she had completed with me, decided to go out on her own and open her own business.

When the session was over and just before she left, she asked me – "*Have you ever considered looking for someone to share your office with*"?

I was amazed and I shared with her my Affirmation.

She then took out of her bag a Journal which she reminded me she used when she was attending the Accredited Diploma. She shared with me that she had begun an Affirmation – "*I am now opening my own Business and my address is in Fitzwilliam Place*".

This was an amazing example of manifesting, where two people were saying an Affirmation, and neither of them knew about it.

We now share our office and enjoy every minute.

This is an example of the power of Affirmations in Manifesting.

Personal Responsibility – Taking Charge Of Your Life

Personal responsibility means taking full responsibility for your life, for who is in your life and how you have ended up where you are today.

Essentially it marks the point where you move away from the drama triangle of blaming everyone else for how your life is at this present moment.

Personal responsibility affects every part of your life. Even if you are in control of your professional life but not your personal life, a niggling feeling will eat away at you.

How Early In Life Do You Take Personal Responsibility?

How early in life do you begin to take personal responsibility depends on individual circumstances.

Everybody's journey in life is different and unique.

Some people are forced to take a lot of responsibility early because of family circumstances, such as young people following a traumatic event, or perhaps where they lose a parent. Consequently, they may take on personal responsibility very quickly.

Some of us don't take personal responsibility for our lives until we get a little older. Generally, it comes with maturity and happens when a person moves from being a child to an adult.

How Important Is It To Take Personal Responsibility In Your Own Life?

Until you take personal responsibility in your own life, you will never be happy and you will never be free, because you will always blame others or events that take place in your life for how things turn out.

So taking personal responsibility is a 'must' for happiness.

You can avoid an area of your life for so long, but anything you resist, will persist until you deal with it.

This area of your life will come up again and again and keep prompting you inside, until you do something about it.

Sometimes, you may allow yourself to become stuck in a career or a relationship, but then blame the institution, the career, or another person.

You may say you didn't know you would arrive at the point you are at now, when you first took the job, or perhaps you may blame it on the person who introduced the idea to you in the first place.

Once you realise and accept it was your own decision and choices that brought you to where you are now, you can free yourself from any blame and begin to take action to change your life.

When you stay in your comfort zone, you are not taking personal responsibility, and for this reason you will not expand, learn or change.

Instead you will become stagnant, and the measure of pain and pleasure in your life is equal, thus there is no encouragement for you to change your life in any way.

You will enjoy no challenge, and you will miss out on the excitement and learning that change brings about, to facilitate your growth and expansion.

Bringing an end to the 'blame game' can be difficult. By you deciding to take personal responsibility, you first forgive yourself for the choices you have made in the past, which will then allow you to look forward to the future.

It is easy to become overly self-critical for actions you may have taken in the past and constantly torture yourself with thoughts such as *'if only I had done things the other way I wouldn't be here now'*. However, blaming yourself has the same negative effect as blaming others, and the main point to remember is that the past cannot be undone. The past is there to teach you lessons for the future and it is in the learning that you can move on.

The Role Of A Coach In Empowering Their Clients To Take Personal Responsibility.

Life coaches work through these types of situations by asking their client whether they thought the choice they made in the past was the right one at that time.

Generally, most clients say at that time, they believed it was the right choice.

Further powerful questions probe the real background to the negative feelings they continue to harbour regarding their past choices, for example:

How has holding on to this belief served you?

In exploring the answer to this question, the client generally realises that their thinking has only served to drain their energies and bring them down over the years.

The coach moves the client forward by asking:

Are you prepared to let go of this habit, this mindset, this self-limiting belief?

By looking at the reality of the situation the client sees what a waste of time and energy it is to hold on to the habit, mindset, or self-limiting belief. By the client becoming aware of this, they are able and willing to move forward.

What Are The Reasons You Choose To Avoid Personal Responsibility?

Often you may choose to avoid taking personal responsibility because it feels like the easiest thing to do at the time.

Taking personal responsibility may require you to take a stand in order to speak up for yourself or take a step outside your comfort zone.

To keep the status quo, you may choose to keep the peace, by doing or saying nothing.

This may occur out of fear of owning up to something, but also you may not want to make a move because the habit of blaming the world and other people for where you are is easier.

Alternatively, you may not even be aware you are playing the '*blame game*' and behaving in this way unconsciously.

What Kind Of A Life Do You Live By Failing To Take Personal Responsibility?

If you are in the world of blame and denial you are unhappy.

You are probably someone who procrastinates regularly, who makes excuses and who generally feels life has nothing more to offer.

Once you are stuck in this way you are not free to live your life to its full potential.

Instead you are living in denial about a part of your life and consequently, you will never be fulfilled.

On the surface you may even feel you are a fraud and living with the "Imposter Syndrome" being tormented with damaging thoughts such as *'if only people knew what I really think, they would not choose to be near me'*.

Not being able to live an open happy life means you don't feel in control of your life.

If you are unhappy with your work but rather than doing something positive about it, you decide to stay, by telling yourself *'How lucky I am to be earning the money I am earning,'* the niggling feeling that you are not being true to yourself will remain with you.

It is like living in conflict with your internal values, where *yes* means *no* and *no* means *yes*; where you tell yourself things are fine when really, they are not.

All of this leads to a lot of negative thinking which can be difficult to live with.

In turn, you could find you cling to various crutches for support, to numb the pain, that allow you to continue living in denial, because you think that depending on these crutches will help the pain go away.

But it will never go away until you face up to what is causing the pain.

Ultimately when you fail to take personal responsibility you will live a life of misery because you fail to deal with reality and you may fall under the control of other people and their beliefs which may not be in your best interest.

What Kind Of A Life Do You Live When You Choose To Take Personal Responsibility?

When you take personal responsibility you are happy with life; you are happy with what has happened in your life and meet each new challenge by welcoming it as an opportunity to stretch your potential.

Even when you make mistakes, you can move on quickly because you take personal responsibility for these mistakes and process them as part of your personal and/or professional learning experience.

Recognising the truth of your situation and acknowledging you must take personal responsibility for it, will prove uplifting, as you realise that the only person who can get you out of whatever dilemma you are in is you.

Once you organise your life in a way that you take personal responsibility for everything in it, you take control and can enjoy the freedom of living a life that is truly inspiring to you.

You will be fully present with what you are doing at any given time and never feel guilty because you have taken ownership of your life.

Of course it can be challenging at times because nobody can be in control 100% of the time as life itself gets in the way.

For example, someone close to you may get sick and there is nothing you can do to prevent that happening.

In so far as possible, it is all about having everything in balance. Sometimes you may need to switch off and just be in the moment.

Being aware that you are taking personal responsibility for your life means you feel very much in control of your actions. You can also enjoy that sense of control in how you respond to situations, in what you say, in where you go and who you keep company with.

Basically you enjoy a general sense of control in all areas of your life and this keeps you growing as a person.

At the root of your existence is your desire to excel and you have your own unique potential. You are born to give your best and not just to become comfortable in life. Your desire is to be stretched and to move towards being the best version of yourself in this world.

When you take personal responsibility you are always learning and contributing to society.

You must be open to learning. No matter how much an expert you may be in your field, there is always a new angle or another concept of the mind that will encourage you to learn more.

Every day is a learning day.

You may meet up with a friend you have not seen for a while, who as soon as you sit down, begins the conversation by blaming the weather for how they feel, or blaming their country for their current situation.

There are certain people who live a life of blame and it could be your sister, your mother-in-law, or a friend.

You could become the brunt of their frustration as they seek to blame you for their poor relationships, levelling accusations such as *'only for you, I would never have met this guy',* even though it was their choice to go out with that person in the first place.

When you walk away from meeting with a person like this you may feel your energy is drained. Their negative attitude can affect you by depleting your energy and therefore it is very important to wean such people out of your life.

The reality is, we are who we hang around with.

Look around at the people in your life and see are they taking full responsibility for where they are and where they are going in their lives.

If they are not, you may want to consider making some changes.

Six

· ·

Procrastination

"Procrastination is the thief of time, collar him"
– A quote from Charles Dickens in *"David Copperfield."*

What Is Procrastination?

Procrastination occurs when you leave something undone and don't do it on the day or the time you are meant to do it.

In other words you don't start what you need to start because you put it off.

You defer or postpone it, often on the basis that you will do it the next day or maybe the next week.

Procrastination is often called the 'thief of time' because you miss out on opportunities as a result of failing to carry out necessary tasks or jobs.

You tell yourself you will do the work tomorrow but then tomorrow becomes another today and you still say you will do it tomorrow.

Consequently, procrastination interferes with the structure of your day, because by failing to complete the necessary tasks as you should, you duck and dive in order to avoid doing them.

This has the knock-on effect of putting your entire day out of kilter which in turn has a direct impact on how you feel and how you perform.

You need structure in your day. Procrastinating on doing the things you should be doing hits the core of your foundation, leaving you with a sense of being out of control.

Procrastination is something you do both consciously and unconsciously. You may not even realise or understand that you are simply postponing something that must be done.

The end result can be, that the issue develops into something really annoying over time, because it may be a job around the home that absolutely needs doing and every time you are reminded that it still needs to be done, this has a negative, niggling effect on you.

More worryingly, procrastination can be extremely draining on your energy resources.

In avoiding doing a task you are subconsciously aware you are not performing at your best and this in turn brings your mood and energy down.

Effectively, you are willing to settle for less and in the process you are letting opportunities to improve and better your life and your situation, pass you by.

The bottom line is, there are 24 hours in the day in which to do whatever it is you choose to do.

How Big A Problem Is Procrastination?

Very few people I know don't procrastinate, whether that is on a small or a large scale.

Regularly I see people who are very functional in their work but then who procrastinate relentlessly at home.

A typical example would be a plumber who never fixes his own sink even though he spends all day fixing other people's sinks.

Or it can arise in your work, where you want to ask your boss for a raise but keep putting it off, telling yourself perhaps you will do it in the afternoon because your boss should be in better form by then. However, the working day is now over and you still haven't asked.

When you leave work and go home, there may then be a displacement of your frustration in the form of aggression against the person you love, which in turn can make life hell for them.

Procrastination is in all our lives but we just pretend not to notice it or acknowledge it is having a negative effect on us, when in fact it can impact on everyone and everything around us.

Constant procrastination about almost everything in your life can become embedded in your personality and develop into a chronic negative habit.

As a result it can be very difficult to train yourself not to behave in a way that feeds your tendency to procrastinate and instead work towards getting rid of this habit from your life.

Consequently a vicious circle ensues where your energy slumps, you do not feel productive, ultimately leaving you feeling lazy and unworthy.

Excuses We Make And Examples Of Procrastination

It is human nature to use avoidance tactics as a means of getting out of doing necessary tasks and we procrastinate on little things as well as big things.

For example, you might indulge in a tea or coffee break as an excuse not to do something, telling yourself that once you have your cup of tea or coffee you will be able to do the job then.

You fool yourself into thinking by taking the break you will be inspired to do what you must do, when really you are simply deferring the inevitable and should just sit down and tackle the work head on.

What you are really doing is lying to yourself!

You are telling yourself the lie that once you have your tea/coffee you will do the work, but you do not. You feed yourself another lie, by saying you do not actually have the time to do it now – but you had enough time for your coffee!

Procrastination therefore, allows you to feed yourself with one lie after another because it is the 'thief of time'.

Another form of procrastination is watching too much TV or rewarding yourself with a TV break in the middle of a task, as an excuse not to complete the task.

You promise to return to the task as soon as the next programme is over but this is not helpful because TV takes you into a world that disconnects you from the world you need to be in and takes your mind completely of the task.

Procrastination also occurs when you put off making appointments you need to arrange, such as going to the dentist or setting the date for your driving test.

Similarly, when you have phone calls to make to colleagues or clients who you may not particularly like, you are often willing to make every other phone call or perform any trivial job just to avoid making the one necessary call.

Or you may avoid replying to emails you should attend to first. You procrastinate by skipping these emails and tending to ones that really are not that important.

This in turn can negatively affect work relationships with colleagues and peers as it can portray you as someone who cannot be depended upon.

Personal relationships can also suffer when you fail to make that call to the friend you need to talk to, or to someone you had an argument with.

The only way to counteract this behaviour is to tackle the job in question instantly.

This means you must make the phone call you dread, or reply to the email you want to avoid, because once you do this, your energy will go up for the rest of the day.

Alternatively, if you fail to do the task, just knowing it is still there waiting for your action, will drain your energy all day because in your mind you know you will that you still have to do it.

The business of networking around work is another area where procrastination can manifest itself if you are someone who tends to make connections but then fail to follow up on further opportunities.

You may go through the motions of swapping business cards and engaging in conversation, but in order to capitalise on your new connection you must follow up with a phone-call but for some reason, you can always find an excuse not to do so, or make that call.

Despite telling people you would love to meet up with them again and continue your conversation, you fail to bring your diary with you to organise a meeting so that the truth of the situation becomes clear – you really do not want or intend to have a conversation.

Procrastination can even happen when you are driving your car and you see that the petrol gauge is on empty but you still refuse to stop and fill the tank.

Instead, you opt to drive to the next town and then suddenly your car stops in the middle of nowhere and you are left stranded because you have no petrol.

This is about not dealing with what is in front of you and telling yourself a different story to the real story playing out, because it is easier to pretend rather than face reality.

Procrastination In The Home

One of the most obvious places procrastination takes place is in the home.

Little things around the house will always need tending to and once you become aware of a job that needs doing, but don't do it, you will be constantly be reminded of it every time you are in the particular part of the house involved.

It is somehow easier to indulge in procrastination in the home, because there is not the same structure as at work - where there may be meetings to prepare for and duties to complete by a certain deadline.

Consequently, rather than looking after the home as well as you could, you might get into the habit of not cleaning properly, or of letting clutter block open spaces.

This freedom in the home can eventually work against you, because procrastinating on all the little jobs will eventually drain your energy and may even overwhelm you if you let the jobs stockpile. You may become very frustrated over time and even want to avoid going home.

Chronic Procrastination And How It Can Lead To Failure

Procrastination can become chronic and life-altering when it is something you do over and over again so that it becomes habitual over the years.

It can affect your career and life opportunities when your procrastination habit means that you leave it too late to apply for that dream job you wanted. Or perhaps you failed to follow up on an invitation because subconsciously you allowed a fear to grow that you were not ready for this opportunity.

Chronic procrastination can also manifest through your tendency to always say "yes" to requests when you really mean "no", which in turn can rob you of the time you need for the really important things in your life, such as your personal relationships.

Or perhaps you are someone who are prone to making last minute cancellations and think nothing about making an excuse as to why you suddenly cannot attend a meeting.

The reality, of course, is, you simply do not want to be there and by letting it go to the last minute, not only do you show you do not value your own time, you also reveal that you have no respect for the other person's time either.

In a close network the word will circulate about this type of behaviour and you will be spoken about in terms of someone who cannot be trusted. Trust is the foundation of any relationship and once trust is broken it can take a very long time to rebuild it and in many cases it may never be rebuilt.

In terms of your professional life, if you don't deliver on a task when you were meant to, and the reason you didn't is simply because you procrastinated, work colleagues will take note of this and won't ask you again.

Over time this may lead to you being side-tracked and overlooked at work, which will result in you missing further opportunities due to your having gained a reputation as someone who does not perform effectively.

Chronic procrastination is exceedingly dangerous, as over time, it can lead you into depression, by feeding into emotions of not feeling worthy.

It is the little voice in your head (the Gremlin) that feeds your procrastination habit, providing excuses as to why you can keep avoiding tasks, for example, by telling you that you are too tired, that it is alright not to do the job or that you will do it tomorrow.

Your tendency to procrastinate can also manifest through certain habits you develop and stick to in the way you live your life. For example, if you are someone who is perpetually late to meetings or events, even though there is no good reason for this to be the case.

A typical scenario could be, that you have a meeting at 6pm on Saturday with nothing else pressing to do on that day, so you decide to spend your day in your dressing gown. Even though you have all day to get ready, you only really start getting ready at 5pm and then find you are in a big hurry to get out in time for 6pm. What stopped you from getting organised in time?

People who leave things to the last minute may behave in this way because there is an adrenaline rush that comes with the need to hurry last-minute preparations and also because they can still congratulate themselves once they do make it to the event in question – even if they were a little rushed or perhaps late in arriving.

A tendency to cram for exams works along the same lines. Although you may have ample time to study throughout the year, you opt instead to leave it all to the last minute.

While again there may be an adrenaline rush attached to this scenario, cramming also brings with it elements of panic and fear that are not conducive to helping you perform at your best during exam time.

Personal Examples Of Procrastination

Example 1

In my own home there was a piece of fraying carpet on the way into the bedroom. I needed to put new carpet down on the spot but for some time, however, I kept putting off this job. The result was that every time I went into the bedroom I tripped on the frayed carpet until it got to the point where it became annoying and dangerous.

Putting it off again and again through procrastination and not doing this simple job only served to drain my energy over and over.

When I finally got the job done, it felt like an enormous weight had been lifted off my shoulders.

I could however have avoided a lot of inconvenience and frustration, had I just completed the job as soon as it needed doing.

Example 2

Several years ago, I was delivering a course on the theme of *Finding the Career you Love* and was very much enjoying working with four different groups of people.

At the same time, I received an amazing invitation from a holistic health company in Greece asking me to travel over and deliver the course.

The invitation came by email and I was delighted when I read it and, of course, was totally up for the challenge.

In the email they requested that I provide a detailed outline of the programme explaining how it would help students and I knew it would take approximately two hours to put this submission together.

Every day I promised myself I would sit down and work on the outline and answer the email but however, I did nothing.

Two weeks went by and I received a follow-up email from the company in which the manager advised me that they had been looking forward to receiving my reply but it had not come.

He continued: *"We waited for you to contact us Mary but because you did not, we had to go with somebody else."*

I have never forgotten that day and the lesson it taught me about how my own procrastination caused me to lose a great opportunity.

The fact is, I really wanted to deliver that course but it was the fear of the unknown that led me to procrastinate on doing the necessary promotional work and following through on the job.

I vowed never to allow such a mistake to happen again and I never have.

What Are The Pitfalls, When You Procrastinate?

There are many difficult lessons life teaches you when you indulge in procrastination, but often you ignore these lessons or just tolerate them to maintain your behaviour.

However, when you miss out on a serious opportunity in your own life, this may form the turning point where you decide you might learn from it and take action to ensure such a thing never happens again.

More importantly, you need to realise that engaging in your tendency to procrastinate does not only affect you, but also everybody around you and everything else you do.

Firstly, it affects the pace of work on a given day because by procrastinating on the first jobs to be done, the rest of your day falls behind.

Over the long term this builds up to a situation where everything important is left on the 'long finger' and your productivity heads towards a standstill, which in turn, affects all those depending on you at work, and the people in your home environment.

In other words, your entire circle of office colleagues, your family, friends and all the people who matter in your life, will be affected.

You will be known as someone who is not performing at full capacity, and instead, operating at a low energy level that serves not only to bring you down but also those around you too.

The Fear That Causes You To Procrastinate

Procrastination is a product of your own resistance and your own fears.

The fear is based around being afraid of where being productive might take you.

Doing the things, you need to do, may lead you on a road that you are not comfortable with.

You are not sure where it will take you if you perform as well as you could.

Being on top of things might move you out of your comfort zone.

You are the product of your belief and value systems, and you allow a tendency to procrastinate to develop, by not believing in yourself.

Sometimes, you are resisting doing something out of a fear of how great you might be. Afraid of your own greatness.

Consequently, you make excuses for yourself and cancel some tasks you want to do, allowing yourself to procrastinate instead.

There is also a general fear of the unknown in procrastination.

The person who procrastinates poses unnecessary questions and scenarios to support their avoidance behaviour, such as: *'If I do go in and take part in this task as I should, what will happen? Will I make a fool of myself?'*

Sometimes the fear is based simply around not believing you are good enough to do something. This is what I refer to as your *'inner gremlin'* filling you with false beliefs.

This gremlin tells you that you are not good enough to consider this particular opportunity and then causes you to think up all sorts of negative self-sabotaging thoughts in order to reinforce your doubts, such as making you pose questions of the type, *'why would I bother starting that, it is much better to stay as I am?'*

Or you might decide, *'I won't apply for that interview (even though I would love the job), because I wouldn't get it anyway.'*

What this is really about is self-sabotaging; settling for less. It is about having lower expectations of yourself, which finds its roots in one of the most common expressions that goes:

"Expect nothing and you won't be disappointed."

What a negative belief this is and yet how many people receive this advice from others in their daily life?

Clearly such *advisers* do not have your best interests at heart.

There are many other external messages you may absorb from different people that serve to feed your internal saboteur.

For example, if you are someone who is working but unhappy and wanting to move to another job, you might receive the advice *'aren't you lucky to have a job at all?' You should be very grateful and not be stupid enough to try and make any change. Don't even think about looking outside for another job.'*

External messages, such as these can be very influential and even more so if the person who is giving you these messages is someone important in your life.

As a result you may opt not to take any action to change your situation. Instead you may decide rather than fulfilling your desire to find more fulfilling work, you will do the opposite of becoming proactive and instead, procrastinate.

In effect you are doing what many people with a tendency to procrastinate do. You are settling for less.

However, behaving in this way will have a detrimental impact on you as a person and in how you continue to perform from there on because you will be forced to acknowledge that inside you there is a niggling feeling that you want more, that you want to do more, that you want a better job or to work for a bigger company and that you want to do something about it.

By denying yourself the freedom and the choice to satisfy this opportunity you are leaving yourself open to becoming frustrated and annoyed, which will ultimately lead you to feeling stuck or blocked in your life, which in turn can develop into a sense of paralysis.

What is happening is that you are going against your value system and that niggling feeling remains with you.

Through coaching you learn what your values really are. You become quite self-aware and this enables you to voice exactly how you feel and what you want.

In this situation, it would mean being able to articulate your need for change; your need to get away; to say *no* instead of *yes* to those who are giving you false advice.

You would be strong enough to say that nobody is going to stop you doing what you know you want and need to do.

When you procrastinate you are entertaining the "Imposter Syndrome" and allowing it stop you from being proactive.

As Marianne Williamson wrote in her poem *"Return of Love"*:

"Our greatest fear of all is how great we are";

"Our deepest fear is not that we are inadequate";

"Our deepest fear is that we are powerful beyond measure".

Different Styles Of Personalities Can Procrastinate More Or Less

We are not born procrastinators. Rather, a tendency to procrastinate is something that develops over time as a bad habit.

How much you procrastinate depends on your temperament. Different temperaments are more prone to procrastination than others.

For example, very detailed and analytical people tend to procrastinate more.

They prefer to leave things on the 'long finger' because they spend too much time analysing and persuading themselves not to do something on the basis that they need to do more research into it first.

Unless you give these people a specific date to have something completed by, they tend not to do it.

However, if they have a date to work towards, they are much more likely to complete whatever the required task is.

What We Can Tell About A Person Prone To Procrastination

It seems to me that people who procrastinate are not happy people. Instead they are just getting by in life and not reaching their full potential.

Often they are people who don't live in the present moment a lot, but who live in the past and how things used to be.

Or they may waste energy terrifying themselves about the future and what might happen in it, becoming afraid of the unknown.

Some people who procrastinate also prefer to live with certainties rather than probabilities, because this gives them an excuse not to do something when actually what a person must do to succeed in life is to be proactive and to take action.

Often it is not possible to have certainties about how things will turn out, but when people choose to be attached to certainties, they will always procrastinate.

Instead of tackling a task head on, they decide, *'I won't do it until I have this or that sorted out.'*

This can affect everything from your personal life to your career, where you may decide, *'I won't start on this until I get that qualification'*, which gives you the excuse to wriggle out of being proactive. Again, this is an example of being unrealistic.

Procrastination can also be used to express a displacement of aggression or a denial of reality.

If you are someone who regularly turns up late for meetings and appointments, clearly you are not being efficient with your time. Therefore you evidently do not value your time. You are lacking the discipline and routine that feeds into the structure – or lack of structure - in your daily life.

If you don't value your time, you don't make the money you need and then a loop develops in your life between power, money and time. You feel bad, annoyed, depressed and frustrated with yourself but you continue to procrastinate and thus stay stuck.

When you don't value your time, you don't value your life, because if you did, you wouldn't be missing out on opportunities.

Again this comes back to being afraid of greatness, so you may constantly manifest this reality through making excuses not to do things.

As a result you are surviving instead of thriving in your life, taking the path of least resistance, standing back and letting someone else go ahead of you.

Adopting this kind of behaviour means you will never realise what you want to realise in your life - self-actualisation – becoming the best you can be.

Not fulfilling yourself will in turn directly impact on how you feel about yourself and how you appear to others.

You may come across as dull and lifeless with little good to say about anyone or anything.

This is simply because internally you feel so frustrated for doing nothing, for not being proactive and efficient with your time, and therefore you struggle to get energised about anything.

Being a proactive person rather than being a person who procrastinates, is linked to being productive, active, and excelling as a person, rather than being just someone who is mediocre.

It is about taking action, about *doing* and not just *being*.

Techniques To Beat Procrastination And Find Your Focus

The best way to tackle procrastination is by starting with the first step, whatever that may be, towards doing the job or jobs that need doing.

Generally, in coaching, I would begin by taking the client through the various areas of their lives, focusing on any negative areas where there is a priority for work to be done.

For example, you may have needed to organise a teaching class but didn't know where to start.

I recommend the best approach is to start by putting an agenda together.

This might be a simple thing such as deciding that the day will open with tea and coffee at 10.30am before the course itself begins at 11am.

Putting structure around the task like this, helps get you into the mindset of completing the task of organising the meeting.

Once you put the opening structure in place in written form, the plan for how the rest of the day can go, will flow more easily.

It is all about approaching the task that needs to be done by taking it one step at a time, starting with the smallest thing you are procrastinating on first and putting a time limit in place by which you will get it done.

What really needs to happen is for you to become proactive rather than passive.

For example, if there is a small paint job that needs tending to in the home, by saying *'I am completing this painting job by this Saturday.'* Setting the date and taking the trouble to go out and buy exactly what you need, will put you in a positive frame of mind towards completing this task.

By tackling one small job at a time in this manner, you build up your inner resources to become more and more productive and efficient in how you run your life overall.

The secret to avoiding a tendency towards procrastination is to always set end dates around everything that needs to be done and to break down big tasks into mini-tasks that can be tackled one step at a time.

Often it is the enormity of a task that can put you off because you are afraid of just how big the job in question might be.

For example, if you have a whole series of assignments to complete by a certain date, you should set targets around when you will complete each assignment one at a time in order to make the deadline. Start with the easiest task first as this builds up in your mind an external reference, that you broke the habit of procrastination by completing this task and then you move forward to the next task.

The process works the opposite to setting goals, where you tend to look at the primary goal you wish to achieve first, and then the next goal after that.

When I am coaching someone with a tendency towards procrastination, I invite them to list everything they procrastinate on in terms of their work-life balance between their job and their home.

This is how you can build your inner resources and change your beliefs and expectations about how you can live your life.

By starting with the little tasks first you are going through the process one step at a time of becoming stronger and more self-reliant.

In regard to the work environment and your relationship with colleagues, an example of how to overcome a tendency to procrastinate could be, that you make a promise to yourself to keep your word on everything.

This means whenever you promise to get back to someone, make contact or follow up on something, you commit to keeping your word and doing the necessary work and following through.

Behaving proactively in this manner will mean you are living up to your work responsibilities and keeping your promise to yourself. You will start to feel a lot better about yourself.

Overall, the best route to tackling procrastination is to learn to become your own observer.

Start by observing your own emotions with regard to how you are behaving and whether this behaviour is serving you well.

For example, if you find at work you fail to speak up at a meeting when a particular person is sitting at the table. First become aware you are doing this; what is the reason you are doing this and how is it making you feel? Then ask yourself how do you want to feel and what can you do to address the situation. This will take some time and might need some coaching.

Your goal is to become proactive by speaking up spontaneously at these meetings and not allowing the presence of the other person to interfere in the natural flow of your thinking around the subject under discussion.

Once you do this the first time, you will experience a sense of achievement that will help you carry through and do it again and again until a new proactive pattern of behaviour develops.

Exercise

How To Counteract Procrastination?

Make a list of all the tasks you need to do but are avoiding doing

Prioritise your list from 1-10

Make a decision to tackle one of your priority tasks today

Write down what you need to do to get the process started

Set a target date by which the task must be completed and commit to meeting this date.

As you tackle the tasks, one by one, begin to visualise yourself being productive in all aspects of your life.

Imagine how it looks and feels to be performing at your best in all that you do.

When you truly visualise yourself in this way and see yourself performing at your optimum and doing exactly what you know you can do, you will also notice you are so much happier and fulfilled living your life in this way.

You realise by completing the tasks you have been avoiding, you can grow and progress in your life.

By Beating Procrastination, Your Life Can Be Very Fulfilling

When you become a person who no longer procrastinates and instead behaves proactively towards how you live your life, you feel on top of the world.

You feel more enthusiastic about everything, more powerful, productive and in control.

The reason you feel this way, is because you are being true to yourself, you are following your values and your goals and doing everything you choose to do.

It is never too late to change and perform at your optimum. This will allow you to live life to the full and never live and suffer with regrets.

Seven

· ·

Coaching In Practice

Who Is Coaching For?

Some people are acutely self-aware and have spent a life-time on self-development. For this reason, they might not require the services of a coach.

Personal & Executive coaching offers a body of knowledge that focuses on the development of human potential at all times. There are already very self-aware; who have worked hard to ensure there is good balance between all areas of their lives and who have succeeded in generating their own high self-worth and as a result they do not necessarily need a coach

However, should such people recognise there is a gap in their life, they are most likely to seek the assistance of a coach?

It also helps those who want a personal or professional breakthrough, perhaps through making a career change.

Coaching may also help people by identifying and developing some talents that may have been dormant all their lives.

It may also lead to someone instituting a new and more beneficial work–life balance; or helps them get ahead professionally; make better decisions; become a better manager/business person etc.

Sometimes, as a successful person you may have lost sight of your values and the whole meaning of life along the way, and consequently you feel stuck. You want to go to the top but just don't know how to get there.

Monetary success does not always equate with happiness or enjoyment at work. You may be earning a high salary, but still feel life is not much fun and not easy. This is because you don't have what you want most, yet because you are successful on the outside, you don't know what to do to achieve this feeling of success internally.

Coaching is designed to tap into unrealised potential and move you forward through setting personal and professional goals that will maximise fulfilment for you and give you the life you really want.

Generally in my coaching practice I find I attract a Clientele of people who want to improve their lives and who perhaps need to work around a few self-limiting beliefs and fears.

This type of client is generally quite successful, however stuck in one or two aspects of their lives.

I find working with this type of client rewarding because what I set out to do in my work is to move people who want to improve, from greatness to brilliance.

Because they know they can fail in their goal perhaps due to a tendency towards procrastination, this is when they opt to go to a Personal & Executive Coach in order for them to be accountable to somebody else to achieve their desired outcome.

In my experience many of those seeking coaching are professionals either looking to change their career, move out of a relationship, or build greater confidence at work.

Coaching can and does help many successful people make their lives even better where perhaps the following scenarios apply:

In monetary terms they are doing well but they may still not be enjoying their work

They are working in a physical environment where they must tolerate certain people who make them uncomfortable

There is no fun in their life and so they feel life is not easy

Despite the financial success, they don't have what they really want most in life

Now that they are successful they don't know what to do next

They have lost sight of their values and the meaning of life.

Who Is Coaching Not Suitable For?

Coaching does not suit people who are sceptics or people who are happy playing the victim and who have no intention of making changes in their lives and moving on.

Anyone seeking coaching in these circumstances might actually benefit from counselling or some other form of therapy instead.

You Must Be Ready To Engage In Coaching

It is very important that anyone presenting for Personal & Executive Coaching actually wants to be there; that they want to focus and get clear about where they are stuck.

For coaching to work, you need to be ready and willing to engage with the process. You must want your life to be looked at and challenged in order to make changes and move on. If you are not open to the process of change, coaching will simply not work.

Coaching is a three-way relationship between client, coach, and the coaching relationship itself. There is a requirement on both parties to invest effort and energy into finding out where things are going wrong and how to go about putting them right.

The client must choose to commit to doing some work to make the required life changes.

It is important to note that the coach never works harder than the client.

I am always challenging clients to reach the best version of who they are.

Picking Up On The Energy

There are a few indications that tell me whether a person who presents themselves for coaching is genuinely interested in coaching.

As humans we are all energetic beings. We vibrate energy to and from each other. Our world revolves around the energy we give and receive. This is evident everywhere in life.

Personally I am very sensitive to energy and can usually pick up exactly how someone is feeling.

I also have very high intuition and often sense and feel things before they happen.

For example, I can automatically feel the energy coming from the other person and know by the way they sit if they want to be here. If they do, they will lean forward and face towards me and listen.

Additionally I can pick up signals from a person's physiology, including their tone of voice. I am aware of how a question is received by my client.

For example, if a client's tone of voice drops low, in their response to a question, I can tell it has impacted badly and I can feel the low energy. This may be because they are in denial about this area in their life and tend to avoid it because it is uncomfortable.

If somebody is sent to me for coaching against their will, it is most likely they won't want it to work in the first instance. I can immediately sense that they don't want to engage in the process of coaching.

The reason coaching can't work if you don't enter it willingly is because the process is not just about you. It is also about the coach and the relationship you both build up between you.

Therefore there is a three-way alliance at play and for it to work both parties must be in agreement. Consequently it is critically important that a person coming for coaching is there of their own free will.

Nonetheless, even in a scenario where someone has come to me involuntarily I have found it is still possible to turn the situation around, because once I explain the process of coaching to that person and outline how it can help improve their situation, they decide to commit.

Interferences In The Coaching Process

There can also be additional pressures that interfere with the coaching process.

For example, if a client arrives for an appointment stressed out because they are late and preoccupied with obstacles that had been in their way during the day, I would conduct a two-minute mindfulness exercise to help them de-stress.

This helps them return to the present moment, where it is crucial their mind must be, because coaching is all about working in the present moment consciousness. It is not about what happened in the past or what is happening in the future. Working in the present moment consciousness is essential because this is where the magic of coaching takes place.

Most People Will Open Up To An Opportunity To Make Their Life Better.

Anybody willing to go to life coaching knows it will be very good for them. The only main competency they need is willingness to change because people who are open and willing to change will also generally be more productive.

Generally, after the first session, most clients leave saying they did not realise it would open so much for them. They report feeling challenged, but in a positive way. There is work to do but they want to do it.

Other clients accept they have been in denial and is now ready to take action.

New Life Process Opens Up For Those Who Engage

For those who genuinely and willingly commit to engaging in the process of coaching with a life coach, a wonderful new life process is set in motion, as follows:

You begin to take yourself more seriously

You start to take more effective and focused actions immediately because you set your accountability with the Coach

You stop tolerating things that waste your time and energy, both physically and emotionally

You create momentum so that results come more quickly and build on each other

You set clear and defined goals that are more exactly what YOU want

When you work with a coach, the coach invites you to work with the SMARTO model and the GROW model. This is to ensure that the goals are Specific, Measurable, Achievable, Realistic, and Time-bound and that the client takes Ownership.

Also, using the GROW (Goal, Reality, Options, Way forward) model we check out the reality of the situation with the client.

We then move forward to the client's options, positive and negative and then we move forward with positive steps with time bounds around each step and then we wrap up.

This process is instrumental to any coaching outcome.

Types Of Clients Who Present For Coaching

It is not possible to describe all types of clients who might present for coaching. However, there are a number of behavioural trends that tend to come up again and again and in broad terms we will look at some of these here; the Victim, the Rescuer and the Persecutor.

1. The Victim

While some clients may be willing to engage in coaching, this does not mean they are readily equipped to deal with the process it entails.

For some people, life is viewed as whatever happens to them during their time on earth is a result of their circumstances and any shortfall has been brought about by someone else - rather than realising that they had a choice and could have done something positive about their situation.

Often the victim feels that the Universe is against them, so they blame everyone from their parents, siblings, wider family, teachers, neighbours and anyone else they can think of, for where they are in their life and all of life's lost opportunities.

If the victim is living in survival mode, where they are barely coping with life and don't have a lot of happiness, coaching can simply be about placing the reality of their situation on the table in front of them. By re-articulating back to them what they are saying and pointing out that nobody is to blame for where they find themselves, the goal is to move them from playing the victim to becoming proactive about their situation and moving forward in a positive way.

For some there may be a reluctance to make this shift because it is easier to stay where they are as a victim because they love the attention they get from adopting this role.

The role of the coach is to guide them towards seeing the positives they will gain from moving forward in their lives, so that they can become aware that each one of us are dealt a pack of cards in our lives, but it is how we play these cards that is important.

VICTIM CASE STUDY 1

Working with a client on the first session of coaching, the client presented in the *victim* mind-set and declared how miserable he was in his job and how he just had to get out of it.

On the second session, he shared with me that he was offered an option of redundancy shortly after our first session, but described this turnaround of events as yet another disaster in his life.

I posed the question to the client, could he instead view this development as an opportunity and see it as a positive in his life. We call this process in coaching *re-framing*.

This is one of the skills the coach can use - to change a negative belief into a positive opportunity.

As we discussed his situation further, the client realised that the real problem was he hated the work he was doing and that the situation presented to him was an opportunity.

He realised the redundancy offer would mean money in his pocket that could be used to actively work towards following his passion and finding a career that he would love.

The redundancy offer was actually enabling him to achieve his full potential.

With a *client who presents as a victim,* the key is to turn the statements they make regarding their situation around, while checking the reality of what they are saying. Example – I may ask a question like - *"where are you getting the evidence to support what you are saying, that everything always goes wrong in your life?"*

Going deeper into the coaching process I then probed further and asked the client to list out examples in his life where everything went wrong as he claimed it did. I made a request of him to ask himself whether he was perhaps generalising, exaggerating or making assumptions along the way.

Following this process I asked him to ascertain whether it really was a fact that everything always goes wrong in his life – or was it perhaps simply a self-limiting belief that he was clinging to from a past experience, that projected this negativity forward – until it became a self-fulfilling prophecy.

After the client realised what he was doing and became very aware this behaviour was not serving him well, we then moved forward together proactively and worked on his new goal of finding a fulfilling career.

VICTIM CASE STUDY 2

Another client I recall working with, who clung to such a victim attitude, reported to me in our coaching session that at work her colleagues were refusing to let her speak. I asked *who was allowing this to happen; who was actually stopping her from speaking?*

These questions stopped the client in her tracks as she admitted she had never looked at the situation like that before. The reality was nobody was stopping her literally from speaking. She was simply allowing it to happen. When work was handed out each week, she would be told someone else would take care of her required quota of jobs for her and not to worry about it.

In this situation where the client was allowing this to happen, the client felt inadequate. I also asked her if her boss was aware of how she felt.

Together we worked on role play over a number of sessions in which she alternately played herself and then her boss, the Project Manager.

We also looked at her family background which revealed she was the youngest of a large family.

During her formative years she recalled how her older siblings had consistently ordered her to keep quiet - on the basis that she didn't know what she was talking about.

This repeated experience led her to develop self-limiting beliefs around her own value and contribution. She felt she could not be assertive and speak her mind because nobody would be interested in what she had to say, thus serving the self-limiting belief that "what I have to say doesn't matter." And the action from this was that the client did not value her own opinion and instead stayed silent at meetings.

Sometime later, following the coaching work this client, she rang to tell me she had spoken with her boss and requested that in future she too be assigned weekly tasks along with her colleagues.

In response her boss disclosed she had not even been aware she was overlooking her.

After our last session of coaching, the client spoke up at the weekly meetings

Over time she was also invited to offer her own ideas, with the result that, instead of leaving her job as had been her original plan when she first initiated coaching, she achieved a promotion and stayed in the job she grew to love.

All of this came about due to a complete turnaround in her self-limiting beliefs, moving away from playing the victim and instead taking personal responsibility for her life.

2. The Rescuer

Sometimes a client shows up and explains their life in terms of playing the role of the *rescuer* – the person who is mothering everyone around them in order to keep all involved happy, resulting in the client feeling exhausted.

The *rescuer* is often the eldest in the family who looks after everybody else, checking whether anyone else would like a cup of tea and pouring it out for everybody.

The reality is they have been playing that role all their life and just don't know how to act otherwise.

In turn people take advantage of those in the role of *rescuer* because they can see they don't value their time.

A pattern develops with the *rescuer* continuing to do what they always did and consequently they have a problem saying no to those who are refusing to be responsible for their own lives.

What the *rescuer* often does not realise is that because they have been behaving in this manner for so long, they are in fact playing the role of parent to their own parents/siblings/co-workers/partners – who they are actually then enabling to play the role of the demanding child.

Once you bring this reality to the attention of the *rescuer* they are then in a position where they can take control of the situation.

They see that by saying *yes* to everything, they may have been feeding their personal need to be popular – but in a way that does not serve them.

All of us have needs and these are neither good nor bad because what really matters is how you meet your needs. You must meet your needs in a way that serves you – not in a way that drains you.

With regard to one particular *rescuer* Client, the girl in question had too much work on her table but was meeting her need to be popular in a way that drained her.

I coached her around saying *no* effectively and valuing her time.

After a while, those people making demands on her started respecting her time and the boundaries around it.

3. The Persecutor

This type of client is more difficult to understand.

You can be the *persecutor* in the role of a mother, a father, sibling, friend, work colleague or otherwise.

It can be about you being in bad form and wanting to annoy someone to the extent that you persecute them.

In general, with a *persecutor,* coaching takes place through the process of role play, where the client discovers by playing the part of the bully and manipulator, behaving in this way makes the other person feel invalid.

I have coached very successful people who were persecuting in their behaviour.

One client who tended to rant, rave and shout but who presented for coaching for an entirely different reason - had an enlightening moment when I described the various types of clients I dealt with.

She realised that through the coaching exercises we did together, that her behaviour was very dominant, displayed bad temper and had a high red flag marking her behaviour resulting in persecuting and bullying work colleagues at times.

Once this client accepted this reality and feedback, she could then act on it in a positive way.

I coached her on how to make requests and ask work colleagues to do something in an influencing - rather than a demanding and disrespectful way, which worked extremely well in practice.

With *persecutors,* they often don't know they are behaving in this way - although colleagues may not be able to recognise this.

For those who are unintentionally persecuting those around them, coaching can work very productively because it requires them to look at the pros and cons of holding on to this type of behaviour. Coaching also reveals the client to themselves and their "Blind Spots."

Generally they come to learn there is another and more effective and pleasant way of communicating and leading.

Everyone at some stage in life will spend some time on the "Karpman's Drama Triangle." The "Karpman's Drama Triangle" consists of: The Victim, the Rescuer and the Persecutor as explained above. However, as you become more self-aware, your goal in life will be to stay off the Drama Triangle as much as possible and be responsible for your behaviour at all times.

Practical Coaching

In general terms of my Personal & Executive Coaching Service, coaching takes place over four sessions.

The reason why it cannot be conducted in just one session is because there is a process involved.

Both the client and the coach engage in this process, which is all about facilitating you to perform by eliminating any fears you might have, which in turn opens the space to allow you get to where you want with clarity, conviction, and purpose.

As a client you decide what area or areas you want to focus on and once you have identified the core area, then together we can work on addressing where the issues lie.

We work together to deal with any blockage that creates difficulty in a particular area of your life at a given time.

Some clients hire a coach to empower them to achieve specific goals, however sometimes they discover there are even greater heights to achieve and remain working with the coach.

Coaching is focused on the client's agenda and continues for as long as the client sees value in it. Focus can be on implementing new skills, changes and goals.

Introduction To The Coaching Session

A typical introductory life coaching session entails the use of the practical coaching tool known as *The Wheel of Life* (explained in detail in Chapter Nine). *The Wheel of Life exercise* enables you to identify areas in your life that may need attention. The coach invites the client to rate each area in the *Wheel of Life* from 0 to 10. 0 being very bad and 10 being excellent. An example of this could be health (physical, mental, emotional and spiritual); your career or personal relationships. Should the client identify an area with a score of 3, however would wish it to be a 9, this is where the coach and client work together to erase the gap and for the client to achieve their potential score of 9.

This intake session is very powerful because it involves taking a practical and in-depth look at the various areas of your life so that there is no glossing over facts.

As a result you will have opened up your unconscious mind and found out perhaps some self-limiting beliefs that need attention.

Following the introductory session, the new awareness awakened may help you realise other self-limiting beliefs that are holding you back.

These self-limiting beliefs are attended to in a practical way, for example, rationalising the self-limiting belief with the client and how it is holding them back. Then with the client's permission, we use positive affirmations to erase the self-limiting beliefs and the wording of which can be decided upon between coach and client.

What I say in coaching is that "Behind every Result, lies a Decision, behind every Decision, lies your Value System and behind your Value

System, lies your Belief System. Your Belief System drives every Result as you are a product of your Belief System".

Coaching Follow Up

In follow-up sessions we revisit affirmations around self-limiting beliefs and focus on a particular area to work on.

The client is given exercises and practical work to do, such as answering questions regarding their competencies, natural skills, and talents.

On the last session you are invited to bring with you, your original *Wheel of Life* chart. We then discuss what you have explored and the goals you have set. A programme of short, medium and long term goals are then set. Short term goals, span from 0 – 6 months; medium term goals span from 6 months to 2 years; and long term goals span from 2 to 5 years.

What is important is that as you reach the end of your coaching process, you have set a forward programme of consolidated goals, over 6 months, 2 years to 5 years. The steps are there and you can achieve it.

Throughout the coaching process you are given tools to help you work on your issues.

The focus is on the positive, using empowering beliefs and affirmations, which are available for you to say to yourself all the time.

It takes 27-30 days to change a habit, so that once you keep giving yourself these positive messages every day, you will find as the weeks roll on, the changes will already have started within yourself.

Additionally you are encouraged to consciously work to internalise your achievements and any compliments or positive feedback you receive in your everyday life.

We also work on valuing your self-worth.

Self-worth is the value you place on the contribution you give to this world.

It is built on all your achievements to date and continues to grow.

For example, you may not be charging enough for your services; perhaps you are not being promoted.

Self-confidence is the value you give to what you do.

Between coaching sessions there is also contact between client and coach. The purpose of this contact is to check on the accountability of the client to himself or herself. The coach will be expecting to hear some positive progress to have taken place in the interim.

The products of the coaching partnership are action and learning, which together create positive change with conviction.

Blind Spots

The coaching process can reveal blind spots for a client. An example might be, someone who sees herself as positive, assertive and results-driven may be surprised to learn that others actually view her as aggressive and demanding.

What you see in relation to yourself may be the complete opposite to what others see when they meet you.

You might think you are very casual, easy going, cool, calm and sliding along in life, while others may see you as lazy.

Another example could be, that while on holidays at a seaside resort, you get up and shout into a microphone, singing at the height of your voice, thinking that you are a great singer, only to discover that other people think you are really bad and it is time you got off the stage.

Coaching is about being entirely non-judgemental. A coach would never point out a person's weaknesses. Instead, the role of the coach is to ask the questions that make you realise exactly how you are - with a view to pinpointing where you could do better.

Coaching Reveals Communication Is Everything

Coaching is also useful for placing the spotlight on communication deficiencies in a relationship where, for example, someone might complain about something a significant person in their life does that annoys them.

The reality is, that people have habits they don't realise they have, but the good thing about habits is they can be changed.

Even the basic interactions between people can be ruled by habits.

For example, one member of a couple who came to me for coaching, revealed to her partner that there was something he did all the time that annoyed her.

The partner responded saying he had never been aware of this before, as she had never communicated to him that this habit annoyed her.

Once they brought this out in to the open they could work on it and move on.

In this coaching scenario what was expected of the other person was verbalised for the first time. Communication is simply so important.

Even basic irritations in a home such as someone always leaving the lid off the toothpaste, can be remedied, once this particular habit is pointed out.

In the absence of communication however, the person who gets annoyed must realise that they have no right to get annoyed with somebody about something they never said annoys them in the first place!

If there are things you didn't tell someone that might improve a situation, how can you expect them to stop the behaviour? This is what we refer to as the "Psychological Contract."

Blockages You May Not Be Aware Of

Everything you do in life is either towards pleasure or away from pain.

When you are confused, you may not be aware of this, or you may have a blind spot about it, or be in denial and insisting everything is fine when evidently it is not.

For example, you could be going through a process of grieving without realising it, passing through the various stages of sadness and anger to reality, before coming to acceptance and then healing.

A client could come to me in an angry state not realising they are in the anger phase of grieving and that is simply another blockage to them in achieving what they want.

When I am coaching a client, I place the reality of their situation in front of them. I then challenge the client to explain what they are basing their beliefs on. Then I ask the client are they living today in past realities and references, which is making them stuck in the present moment.

For example, you may present with a story that you claim to be a fact, when really it is based on one past experience only. You are making it out to be a fact when in fact it is only a belief about that one experience, or a false reality. It could also be a self-limiting belief.

Moving away from past realities to facing up to what your reality is now, helps you move forward towards taking personal responsibility for your life.

The Fundamental Coaching Tool - The Wheel Of Life

Sometimes people who are interested in coaching are reluctant to engage in the process because, even though they want to grow in some way, they cannot articulate exactly where it is they want to generate improvement.

If you are unsure whether coaching is something that might help you in your life, the best way to find out, is to discover exactly how happy and fulfilled you are in all areas of your life.

One of the most useful coaching tools designed to ascertain a person's life situation is called *The Wheel of Life*. This simple but extremely effective visual tool can be used to help identify where the gaps appear that need attention.

The *Wheel of Life* therefore, is a fundamental coaching tool that you can use as a first step to empower and improve your life.

The *Wheel of Life* constitutes a basic questionnaire that challenges you with regard to the various areas of your life.

The visual *Wheel of Life* representation covers eight areas of your life, providing a holistic overview that allows space to focus on the following:

- ❖ Career
- ❖ Relationship/significant other
- ❖ Personal growth
- ❖ Fun/recreation
- ❖ Family and friends
- ❖ Health
- ❖ Physical environment at work/home
- ❖ Money/finances.

Examining these various areas will provide a general picture of your life and provide a practical method for obtaining an accurate overview.

There are also additional *Wheel of Life* tools that can be targeted for specific coaching areas.

For example, I also use a business *Wheel of Life*, which looks at Management Competencies; Time Management skills; Team Work skills etc.

The client must score themselves in all those areas for us to prioritise the number one area for coaching.

Commencing The Wheel Of Life Process

In order to get the *Wheel of life* coaching process started, you are required to take a helicopter view of your whole life as it is today, covering all areas from personal to the professional, in accordance with the eight areas as specified.

The focus will not be on tomorrow or yesterday but on how you feel right now about each area in your life.

You will be asked to score each area, not just in terms of success, but in terms of how happy and fulfilled you are in each area.

Completing this part of the exercise will then identify areas where the score is low, perhaps due to some fears, doubts, denials or resistance that may apply.

This exercise can prove very revealing. For example, while someone may be successful in their career, and rate their success at a level of 10 out of 10, in the work they are doing, the physical environment at work could be rated at a far lower score, thus affecting the overall happiness and fulfilment in this area.

Once you have rated how happy and fulfilled you are in each area of your life on a scale of 1-10, it becomes clear the areas where the mark is at 9 or 10 means you are very happy in relation to these aspects of your life and don't require coaching around them. Those areas marked at 4 or 5 however might indicate you are stuck in some way and you want to move on from this.

Wheel of Life Exercise

Wheel of Life

Scale of 1–10

- Examine the level of happiness and fulfilment in each area on the Circle of Life.
- Where are you now today?
- Where would you like to move to?

CIRCLE OF LIFE

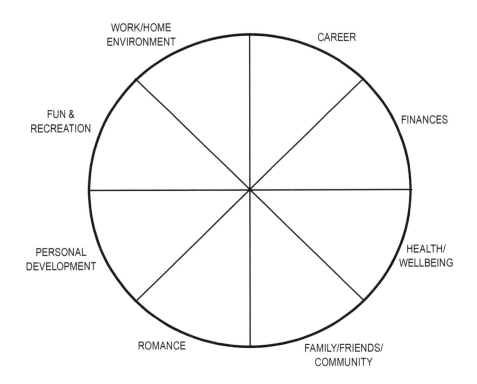

Revealing The Client To Themselves

As you continue to use the *Wheel of Life* coaching tool, the coach can move the process forward by having you ask questions of yourself that assist you in providing the correct rating which in turn can uncover new areas where coaching can help.

As a result of the probing you may realise things about yourself that you were not fully conscious of before.

Here are examples:

- You may discover you are someone who wants to reduce your weight by two stone.
- You may have a professional goal, such as to achieve a promotion at work.
- Perhaps you want to master driving after many years of procrastination.
- Maybe you are simply seeking personal growth – or a fulfilling relationship.
- You have a business idea you want to develop but just don't know how to get started.
- In all of these scenarios coaching can help.

Working To The Client's Agenda

It is always the client's decision as to what area they want to work on.

Therefore, what matters in coaching is that you are always working to the client's agenda.

However, sometimes the client wants to avoid a particular area of challenge, due to denial, or discomfort. Over time, as trust develops in the coaching relationship alliance, generally the client is willing to return to the challenged area and work on it once they feel ready.

Deciding to work on a particular area gives the client a focus, which immediately changes their behaviour for the better.

The Importance Of Powerful Questions

The power of questions in coaching is fundamental to the process, and as coaches we view questions as the most powerful tool.

The reason you might be reading this book today is because of the questions you have asked yourself and because of the questions you are afraid to ask yourself.

When you are ready to both ask and answer the necessary questions, you are on your way to move forward in a positive way.

You will always find that the answers to your questions come from inside of yourself.

It is through the power of questions the coach asks the client, that allows moments of transformation to take place.

As a coach, when I ask you the questions that perhaps you have not been able to ask yourself, the gift of your new life is set in motion because you have finally started to listen.

As the title of this book states – *"Life begins when you are ready to listen"*.

Answering the questions that need to be asked means that you as the client must go inside and take ownership of your situation, of where you are, where you want to go, of the fact you are unhappy or perhaps feeling lost or in a rut.

Searching internally for the answers, causes a shift to take place in which you listen to what is being revealed and start to take personal responsibility for where you are today.

Once this transformative process is initiated you begin to move away from the "Drama triangle of your life", where up to now you may have been blaming the people around you, the culture you grew up in and everything else you could think of, for why you are where you find yourself today.

Coaching For Personal Growth

The two main areas where clients come to me for coaching, are career and personal growth.

Almost everyone I have worked with, includes personal growth in their goals, which can mean working on a lack of confidence in career or personal relationships.

Personally, I can relate to this because at one time in my life I ran a very busy restaurant which was a great business success but unfortunately, I hated my work.

While I won awards and would have marked my career area at 9 out of 10 in terms of success, I would only have marked my happiness and fulfilment in this area as a 2.

There can be a big difference between success and happiness.

When I work with clients in the area of personal growth, I include a number of areas as follows:

- Self – Esteem
- Self-worth

- Self-confidence
- Self-concept

Assessing A Client

In order to find out how open and willing a person is to learn and grow, I ask a number of questions:

- *Where are you confident in your life?*
- *Where are you not confident?*
- *Rate your self-esteem on a scale of 0-10.*
- Where a client scores themselves low, I would ask *the reason for the low score.*

The client might tell me about something that happened to them in the past that affected their self-esteem and we would then begin the coaching process from this point.

Self Confidence Rises And Falls

It is a matter of fact that our self-confidence and self-esteem fluctuates from time to time.

We are born with our self-esteem at 100% but as we get older, primary impressions and our environment affect us.

Self-confidence from a career point of view relates to how confident you are in your *ability at* work i.e. how well you can do your job.

Self-worth is the value you place on your contribution.

Then you have Self-concept, which is how you believe other people see you.

There are many parts to a person and generally in terms of Self-concept, there is a four-fold theory to each person's personality.

I refer to the *"Johari Window Exercise"* below, by *Joseph Luft* and *Harry Ingham*.

- **OPEN PART** – which relates to how you see yourself and others see you (for example, that you are outgoing, an extrovert);
- **HIDDEN PART** – for example, you might be a diabetic but on a first date with someone you might not reveal this.
- **UNOFFICIAL HIDDEN PART** – for example, you might head up a department at work but when you get home your fantasy is to go up to the attic to play with your toy train set; or it could be something more serious – e.g. you could be a criminal and you share this with nobody.
- **BLIND PART** - is what you don't see about yourself that other people see - for example, you may believe you are a great Karaoke singer but nobody else would agree! They might think *why does she not know she is really bad at singing?*

  Or you might walk through the office and behave very aggressively but think you are being assertive; or you might consider yourself to be laid back but others regard this as laziness.
- **DARK PART** - this refers to the part of you where the light has not been shone- your potential; it can be an area you have not discovered yet and coaching can help to reach this potential.

Sometimes in personal growth coaching I could be working with the client in one or more of these areas.

Once again, I would establish where the real issue lies using powerful questions – and then I would rationalise the client's responses.

For example, where a client might say they are very bad at a particular job, I would ask:

Who says you are very bad at this job?

Have you an example of where you are bad in this job?

Many people give a lot of their attention to comparing themselves to others in a negative way. However, very often I find that there is a self-limiting belief present which needs attention.

Lacking In Confidence

When you lack confidence, this can be due to a mistake you have made and did not deal with it properly, resulting in a feeling of failure.

The difference between failure and success is how you deal with mistakes.

When you make a mistake, take time to reflect on it, however stay stuck and not move on, this is failure.

When you make a mistake, reflect on it, and *"Move on"* with the learning as a positive going forward to your future, this is success.

If you are someone who defaults quicker to thinking more about what you did wrong than what you did right, your tendency will be to focus on your mistakes, which will lead to your self-confidence going down.

This is because you are creating doubt and doubt creates failure. Similarly focusing on mistakes keeps you doubting yourself and then you go on to manifest failure as you attract what you think about.

Building Confidence

Clients often come for coaching around confidence and self-esteem. They believe they are not getting a promotion or some recognition they feel they deserve.

Confidence goes up and down but if people compare themselves to others on a continuous basis, they will lack confidence because they are feeding the self-limiting belief – *"I am not good enough."*

To overcome this, I would coach them on focusing on being their best, giving their best and giving their energy and attention to thinking along these lines.

In doing this, they move away from focusing on situations and people outside their control.

I work on building up their confidence by recalling what they have achieved in the past in order to remind them of their own greatness and to empower them to let go of irrational beliefs.

I invite the client to list all their achievements in their life and in so doing they often realise *I have achieved a lot more than I thought I had.*

The reference to the past helps to build their confidence, because when they think "I *have done this before*" they realise they can do it again. The client can now believe they have the resources to overcome any challenge.

Self-Help Measures To Expand As A Person

You can also help yourself grow in self-confidence as a person through expanding your horizons and opening to new experiences.

For example:

- attending workshops
- reading more
- engaging in further education
- travel

Travel opens your mind to new cultures and to doing things differently. Additionally, you can work on your own natural areas of interest to expand your horizons.

Moving out of your comfort zone to engage in new activities means you will be around people and interacting with them. This in turn will help you get to know yourself better.

You can grow in so many ways and everyone has different pathways they can choose to follow.

For example some of you may want to learn more about the spiritual world, philosophy and psychology.

We are all drawn to different things and have our own particular interests.

What is important is that we are constantly growing as people through learning.

Once you are learning about something you love, you are truly on the path of expanding.

Exercise

How To Build Confidence

To build your self-confidence and celebrate your greatness I recommend two basic exercises.

1. List out your achievements – making a note of everything you have achieved in your life so far.

This is important and useful because we tend not to own our achievements. But when you write an achievement down on paper you claim it, name it and own it. Then the unconscious mind feels proud.

2. Make a gratification list, noting down everything you are grateful for.

Be sure when completing this exercise to take the time to remember and include everything you are thankful and grateful for.

The moment you begin the exercises, you are already building up your self-worth and self-confidence because by thinking about what you have achieved and what you are grateful for, you move to a place of high energy, which enables you to manifest and achieve more very quickly.

Ten

. . . .

Career Coaching

As a coach I guarantee to empower clients to achieve clarity around their career and to work towards new goals with conviction and action.

I have many clients I like to work with but my preferred speciality is in career change. This is because I am passionate about this area, given my own personal experience of having changed career several times.

Generally, there are four types of clients who show up in relation to career change.

1. The Clients who are stuck in the "Comfort Zone" where the pain of the work they are doing equal the pleasure of the money they make which gives them a fulfilling life outside their work. The pain and pleasure are equal.

2. The Clients who hate their work, however love the physical environment.

3. The Clients who love their work, however hates the physical environment.

4. The Clients who like their work, however have a niggling feeling that they are not reaching their potential in what they do.

Client Type No.1

This client is someone who may not appear to have a problem at all because they are working in their comfort zone. They are very successful in their job to the point where they can do it with their eyes closed and the money they earn gives them a fulfilling lifestyle outside of work.

However, a problem arises because the person knows they are not *entirely* happy at work and that something is missing. They need to find a way to move forward, but because there are so many positives to their situation outside of work, they may be reluctant to take that step.

The duty of the coach is to empower the client to identify and make the necessary change that will improve their situation.

It must be through the client's own conviction that they decide to make this change, and to empower them to make this happen, can be very challenging for the coach.

Whatever takes place in the process of coaching, the coach must always be mindful to work in accordance with the client's own agenda.

Client Type No. 2

This client is in a brilliant job but they hate the work.

However, they love the people, the physical environment, and conditions of employment. This person needs to make a fundamental change in regard to the actual work they are doing.

While again this is a tough challenge, through a process of coaching they will realise that life is not a 'dress rehearsal' and that working in a job they hate not only affects them but usually it affects family, friends and others around them.

Therefore in this situation, happiness is restored when that person finds a fulfilling career that they love.

In the long term, the work is not the work they want to do so they will eventually feel irritated, because they are likely not being challenged enough. Eventually they will take action once they go to coaching.

Client Type No. 3

This client is someone who loves the work they are doing, but not the people, the place, or the conditions of employment.

This may be because they are been bullied or the physical environment/ working conditions are not suitable.

However, no matter what coaching is carried out, sometimes the client might realise that there is no way to change the people/physical environment or conditions of employment.

This client then needs to make up their mind that they must either move location within this company or change career.

Client Type No.4

This is where the client inwardly knows they can do their work, with their "eyes closed." They like their work, however have a never-ending niggling feeling that there is more to life than the work they are doing.

They feel that they are not reaching their full potential.

Once they work with the process that I have developed in Career Change, they always receive clarity and move to finding a fulfilling career by getting promoted or moving to another Company.

Small Changes Deliver A Positive Effect

A client may come to coaching because they want to change their career. Sometimes it won't require taking a quantum leap to rectify their situation in the work place. It may be that making a small change can have a very positive effect.

For example, the client may realise they were not proactive or taking personal responsibility in their job and consequently drew little enjoyment from it.

A client I coached in this situation, spoke to her boss in an assertive manner for the first time, shared her ideas and asked to be consulted in the future. Following this behavioural change, the client was successful in achieving a promotion and then decided to stay in her job.

Clearly this was simply a case of poor communication between parties.

Job Resentment And Redundancy

As a coach I also work on moving people from the state of resentment to acceptance, e.g., they may resent going into work and detest every minute of it but then suddenly they lose that job and are made redundant.

I invite such clients to look at the 'pros and cons' of their new situation. Through the coaching process, they come to realise that the 'pros' are higher than the 'cons' and see it as an opportunity to have the time and money to do what they are passionate about.

Losing their job, facilitates them to do something they have long dreamed of, such as going back to college to train in an area of interest.

The client begins to see things with a different mindset and attitude. They are moving from resentment to acceptance.

CAREER COACHING CASE STUDY

One lady I worked with in business had to make a lot of different choices, however what she wanted most of all was to be true to herself and what she loved doing.

We looked at how each of the business options she was involved and checked which ones were fulfilling her. After going through the coaching process, she decided to resign from certain areas and to dedicate herself fully to the one main area she loved working in.

As a result she set herself up in an entirely new business and has been thriving ever since.

Subsequently, a friend who was so impressed with the change in her working life and her newfound state of happiness, also came to me for coaching.

She realised that her friend's happiness had resulted from doing the work she loved and she too, wanted to find the work she would love to do.

With both clients I used my career coaching process and empowered them to manifest their future careers in the work that they would love to do. Both clients agree that the outcomes from the coaching process have been extremely rewarding.

Achieving Your Work And Business Goals

Primarily in career coaching, I work with clients on a one-to-one basis to help them achieve their career goals.

Coaching takes place over four sessions and in the first session we work through the *Wheel of Life* process which may additionally help the client discover other areas in their personal, professional, home, and romantic life they may wish to work on later.

For example, perhaps the client is also seeking a fulfilling relationship. It is useful to record this information so that once the career coaching finishes, the client can come back and can re-visit the *Wheel of Life* and look at the other goals that may need to be taken care of.

There are lots of questions I ask throughout coaching that drill down through the detail of the client's working life, to help them think creatively and acknowledge their big dream.

The reality is, once the client receives clarity - the '*how*' regarding getting there is easy, because it is all about strategy after that.

Generally, I find that once the client arrives at the point of clarity surrounding their goals, everything moves forward brilliantly.

At the end of coaching, clients leave with goals to achieve within six months to two/five years.

There are some clients who might show up against their will, perhaps having been sent by management at work.

Generally, I can work with these clients and still get them to where they want to be. This is because, as they engage with the coaching process, they see how it can benefit them in their work and in their personal lives.

The client is therefore ready to open and follow the steps. It is then a case of *when the 'student is ready the master appears.'*

Over the four sessions I empower the client to challenge their negative mindset in the areas they are stuck in, form a positive mindset, and act. Most of my clients achieve clarity with a consolidated set of goals at the end of the coaching sessions.

Through coaching I guarantee my clients to achieve clarity and it is up to the client to act and take personal responsibility.

Career coaching covers a wide spectrum of job and work issues. I invite you now to look at how a real-life career coaching session takes place in practice from beginning to end.

The Coaching Process For Career Change

Session One

___

Exploration

___

In session one with you as a client, my focus would very much be in exploratory mode, where we would look at how things are progressing in your whole life by looking at each section in the *Wheel of Life*.

After we have had a preliminary discussion on the eight areas, we would then focus on your main area of interest i.e., their career.

If you as the client, is a young business person, I would begin by asking you the following:

Can you provide me with a summary of every job you have worked in since leaving school or college.

Exercise

___

Ask Yourself The Same Question And Take Some Time To Include All The Details In Your Answer

___

Following this, I would present you with a series of questions to ask yourself around your working life. This would be targeted at checking out your mindset, looking at what you believe is working for you and what is not working for you.

What I am exploring is, whether you the client may be in denial or in fear of anything and whether you have the confidence to find another job. Or perhaps you may discover that you are more suited to self-employment.

Another exploratory question I would ask you is:

What have you achieved in life that you are most proud of?

EXERCISE

Ask Yourself The Same Question And Take Some Time To Include All The Details In Your Answer

This question is important because some people don't own their own achievements and as a result of that, their self-worth and confidence is quite low.

I would invite you to write down what you have achieved to date, so you can see all your work achievements right in front of you.

Following this, I would ask you to look at any job you have worked in before that you disliked so much that you would never do it again.

This reflection is important because we are working on what you want and therefore not prepared to waste any time on what you most definitely do not want.

Further Powerful Questions For Exploring

Other questions I would pose at this exploratory session would be to ask you:

Where do you think your talents lie – physical, interpersonal and/or intellectual, i.e. problem solving?

Exercise

Ask Yourself The Same Question And Take Some Time To Include All The Details In Your Answer

Next I would present you with the following scenario:

If you were unemployed tomorrow and realised you had no job to go to, what organisation would you look at, or consider working for?

I would look at this in detail with you and through further questions, I would ask you to describe the following:

What size would the organisation be?

Would it be a for-profit or not-for-profit organisation?

Where would it be located?

Exercise

Ask Yourself The Same Questions And Take Some Time To Include All The Details In Your Answers

By actively exploring these possibilities and looking at the idea of a suitable job in detail, you can begin to answer these important questions from your own perspective.

This in turn will help you become aware of any doubts or self-limiting beliefs in your path, which I would then invite you to bring to the next session for discussion.

Session Two

Identifying Self-Limiting Beliefs

In the second session I move to dealing with any self-limiting beliefs you may have.

In order to initiate the process, I would ask you to list all of your fears and doubts.

Once we look at these, I would work with you to compose some positive affirmations around these self-limiting beliefs, because to move forward in the coaching process, you need to move into a positive mindset.

At this juncture any self-limiting beliefs you may have around your work would become evident.

For example, you may realise you are generous to the extreme in your work, to the point where it has become a negative in your life. The end result is you are agreeing to take on too much work. This results in you not valuing your time and allowing other people take advantage of you and causing you to become overwhelmed.

The challenge for you here would be to introduce new boundaries with regard to your time and your working practice.

This would entail you learning to say *yes* and *no* with regard to work requests, in a way that takes into consideration how you value your time.

In this scenario, it may also be necessary to work with you on any need that is feeding this behaviour. For example, it may be your need to be popular that is serving this need in a way that drains you and lessens your self-esteem.

It is important to realise that needs are not good or bad, it is how you fulfil them that matters. Should you serve them in a way that drains you, it is negative, however when you serve them in a way that fulfils you it is positive.

I would spend time with you working on how you can serve the need to be popular in a way that fulfils you. Much of this work would be on your self-esteem/self-acceptance and self-worth. This would lead to you learning to value your contribution and learning to say 'no' in an assertive manner.

Coaching requires clients to ask powerful questions of themselves.

I would end this session by asking you to take away some important career questions to answer in preparation for the next session.

These powerful questions will bring you back in time to what you used to love to do, the subjects you loved in school and the after-school activities that made the you feel so fulfilled.

Session Three

Moving From Negative To Positive MindSet

No action takes place and no change can happen without emotion. In coaching I empower the client to tap into their own emotions. The objective is to move the client from a negative to a positive mindset.

In this session I would invite you to answer some more powerful questions designed to help you to make this shift.

To do this, you must move out of your comfort zone and identify the negative and the positive areas in your career. The reality about acting from your comfort zone is that you are acting from a place where there is pain and pleasure in equal parts and it is this trade-off that keeps so many people stuck in a rut.

Most jobs have an element of pain, but there must be some element of pleasure that outweighs the pain keeping the client there, otherwise the client would have moved on.

For example the team around you could be great but the physical environment and terms and conditions could be painful. Once the pain gets greater than the pleasure of working there, you seek to move.

An example of this could be where a client comes for coaching because they hate their job. This is the pain element.

However, the fulfilling lifestyle the client enjoys outside of work because of the money they earn in the job, is the pleasure element and naturally they will not be willing to give this up easily.

Unless the pain becomes greater than the pleasure, they may decide to tolerate this situation to their retirement.

Therefore they are in their comfort zone and may never leave. They are there until they retire and consequently are living for their pension and not their passion.

Powerful Questions To Ask Yourself

I would ask you to think about the week ahead in your job and describe what thoughts are running through your head on a Sunday night thinking about the week ahead at work.

Exercise

Ask Yourself The Same Question And Take Some Time To Include All The Details In Your Answer

---

This exploratory question can be amazingly revelatory because it provokes strong reactions from anyone unhappy in their job.

Some clients hate even entertaining this question and tell me they simply detest ever having to think of the week ahead.

Example – *"I am like a zombie watching the clock on Sunday evening, dreading the end of the weekend and then for the rest of the week at work, I live for Friday and the next weekend."*

The client who admitted the above was so miserable in her work she did not want to engage with the exercise at all. However, I was able to offer assurance that there was a reason for going through this process because there is a balancing scenario to follow.

The balance comes in the form of the second half of the question which asks:

What do you want your working life to be about?

Exercise

Ask Yourself The Same Question And Take Some Time To Include All The Details In Your Answer

---

Powerful Questions Around Your Comfort Zone

To continue the pain and pleasure analysis I would ask you to consider where your comfort zone lies by answering the following question.

List the elements of pain and pleasure in every job you have worked in including the present job.

Exercise

Ask Yourself The Same Question And Take Some Time To Include All The Details In Your Answer

---

This is a complex question that requires you to go back in time and examine every job you have been in until now, looking at the pleasure and pain.

As we go through this analysis together I would see you starting a process like a rolling stone gathering moss.

What this entails is you looking back and noting the good and bad in previous jobs.

You would identify trends running through each job and come to realise what you do not want and what you really love to do.

In this analysis therefore, you would move from pain to pleasure and out of this confusion comes the clarity that you seek.

In essence, it is necessary to look at what you do not want, to find out what you do want.

Powerful Questions Around Your Life Purpose

Another powerful question I would ask you to consider is as follows:

When have you previously felt 'on purpose' in your life, both personally and professionally?

EXERCISE

Ask Yourself The Same Question And Take Some Time To Include All The Details In Your Answer

---

It is important to consider both the personal and the professional aspects when dealing with this question.

This is because when you are 'on purpose' doing the work you love, you are in a space where you are not clock-watching or thinking of what is coming next.

Instead you are totally in the moment, loving what you are doing to the point you would be willing to do it for free.

Therefore both personally and professionally you feel 'on purpose'.

When clients are asked this question, some might say the only time they felt 'on purpose' was when they were answering questions and providing information for people; or others might say there is nothing in my work that ever makes me feel I am 'on purpose'.

I recall one client who responded to the question by saying she had never felt 'on purpose' in her work in the corporate world. The one time she really did feel 'on purpose' was when she was taking photographs. Her Dad would say to her – *go off and take photographs because you are always so happy when you do.*

This past client is a famous photographer today.

Powerful Questions Around Your Role Models

Another powerful question I would ask you to consider is as follows:

Who do you know that lives a life of integrity and purpose?

Exercise

Ask Yourself The Same Question And Take Some Time To Include All The Details In Your Answer

The reason for this question is because we all need an external reference to keep us motivated when we are on our career journeys. We need role models.

When we admire someone, it is because they are mirroring back to us what we already have inside ourselves that we might not have explored or done anything about. They are mirroring to us our true potential that sometimes we have yet to discover.

Powerful Question Around Your Career

Another powerful question I would ask you at this point would be the following:

If you knew you had six months to live and you were feeling good and healthy, how would you spend those six months working?

Exercise

Ask Yourself The Same Question And Take Some Time To Include All The Details In Your Answer

---

The first reaction to this question is generally incredible. Some clients declaring of course they would not work at all in such a scenario. Instead they would spend their remaining time on a cruise ship or holiday with friends and family around them.

I would continue to probe this area by challenging you as follows:

If you were doing the work you loved during these last six months of your life, what would that work be?

This question provokes the answer to their situation for some clients - but not for others, because it all depends on how a client views their time.

For example, some clients live in the moment while others tend to live in the past or maybe the future.

Some live more for the future and are great planners.

CASE STUDY - RETIRED WORKER

An example of a client I coached through a session on the six month question was a retired worker, who expressed a desire to still be in a job she would enjoy and where she could give back and contribute to other people.

In response to how she might work for the last six months of her life, she said that during her career as a teacher, she had regularly attended a practitioner for reflexology treatments. She had grown to love reflexology and often thought about being able to offer this service to her friends.

My next question was:

If you could qualify as a reflexologist in six months, would you?

At this the woman's eyes lit up and she realised that training to become a reflexologist was exactly what she wanted to do.

She enrolled in the reflexology course and the following year she qualified. Today she has a thriving reflexology practice and offers some of her clients reflexology as a gift.

Powerful Question Around Your Ideal Job

A final powerful question to consider at this point is:

If you knew you could not fail, what work would you love and choose to do?

Exercise

Ask Yourself The Same Question And Take Some Time To Include All The Details In Your Answer

---

This is always the last question I ask a client to consider, however the previous questions must all have been completed before this question.

By following the process in this way, you will have identified the pattern in your working life, highlighting where the positive and negative components exist and now leading you to identify what course of action you would like to take.

With this question I would invite you to imagine your passion and the work you would love to do. I use a Metaphor *"The Genie in the Bottle"* and invite you to imagine the Genie is jumping out of the bottle. The Genie is saying *"I'm putting failure away in to a drawer and I ask you to write down and record in great detail everything about the work you would love to do, now that failure is not an option"*.

You would provide me with three or four different choices. As the coach, I would leverage one choice against the other until you receive clarity.

From here I explore the various options you are considering, looking at your number one choice and then the nearest alternative and at the same time honing down to exact details.

My personal journey to loving the work I do.

A personal example from my own life, highlights for Clients exactly how useful this process is. Earlier in life, I worked in the restaurant business and was totally miserable. To find my fulfilling career, I attended workshops ran by Nick Williams, read every book on Career Change that was available. In this process, I answered every question that I have shared with you

Answering the last question, I wrote down my vision on paper, not believing one word of it. On the basis that I would be guaranteed I would not fail using the Genie metaphor, I wrote what I would love to see myself doing. I was on a stage, empowering and coaching 200 people, talking about change, wearing a red suit. I did not even know about coaching at this point.

Five years later, after I had changed career and moved into coaching, I was asked to deliver workshops on stress and coping with stress in Belfast, Cork and Dublin.

I had already delivered workshops to small-to-medium sized groups in Dublin and was in Cork in the Metropole Hotel when one of the organisers asked me. How are you in talking to a large group of people?

I replied that it would be no problem to deliver my talk to a large group. They arranged a bigger room for the workshop to hold up to 200 people – at least 100 more delegates than I had originally been advised would attend.

In the run-up to the workshop I remember saying to myself, "OK, I'm doing all this work so now I'm going to treat myself to a new suit to wear in front of the large crowd on this occasion".

As I put my hand on a red suit to try it on in a boutique, the thought entered my head, 'I am now wearing my red suit, standing on a stage, and talking to 200 people.'

This was exactly the scenario I had written about in the answer to the last question at the end of my coaching process.

My story is therefore an encouragement to others, that if this could happen to me, it can also happen to you.

My dream became a reality.

It is all down to your belief system.

A Time For Reflection

As session three is such an intense one, in which you have to consider powerful questions that require you to recall deep-rooted memories and experiences from an earlier working life, I generally conclude this session by allowing for a period of reflection.

I would ask you to go through all of the questions and to come back to me with well thought-out answers.

As well as providing answers you may also have a few ideas with regard to the final question about your dream job.

Usually, I would ask a you to take 2-3 weeks to conduct this work. It is at this stage that you become accountable and committed to yourself, to me and the process.

You must research everything you need to research; explore anything you need to explore and do everything you agreed to do in order to move from where you are to where you want to go.

Exercise

Allow Yourself Time To Reflect On Your Answers To The Powerful Questions, And See What Moments Of Clarity You Can Arrive At.

Session Four

Final Session

The fourth and final coaching session revolves around the client having researched and carried out all the steps they agreed to commit to.

Having considered your options since the previous session, you come back to me with answers and clarity about what you want to do.

Some might decide to go back to college, so education may become their primary focus.

Others will want to put into action a plan that will see them achieve their business dream, perhaps over the space of the next six months to two years.

During this final session I would ask you to look at the number one career preference you have decided upon and we would examine how you might get from where you are to where you want to go.

To help move you forward, I would suggest the following scenario:

Let us pretend, I meet you in four years from now and you are doing exactly what you love to do in your career. Describe to me in one sentence, what work would you be doing.

Exercise

Ask Yourself The Same Question And Describe Your Answer In One Sentence

Once you can name with clarity what you would love to do, the focus then moves to defining the strategy of how you are going to get there. You are seeking to move from where you are to what your dream and passion is.

If you find that your number one choice is not realistic, we then look at your alternative option and amazingly, sometimes your alternative choice becomes your number one choice.

For example, if a client finds because of their research that it is not feasible to work for themselves as planned, they may decide to still work in the same industry in an alternative way, which in the end can prove just as fulfilling because it still meets the heart of who they are.

Alternatively, a client's reality could be that they have a big mortgage to pay which means they are not able to act straight away. In this scenario I would encourage the client to work in their field of interest in some way, even in a voluntary capacity. There is always another way to get into their field of choice.

> ***When someone loves the work they do, it will be evident to everyone around them, because these people shine and are remarkable.***

When a client enters the field that they are passionate about, they shine and are noticed. The client starts connecting, focusing, and attracting the people they need and want into their life to progress with their career.

For example, you will always gravitate towards a hairdresser or a coffee-shop owner who loves what they do – because it will be a pleasure to be around them and you will receive the best from them.

People always notice people who love the work they do and respond to them very positively. I believe you only excel in life when you do the work you love.

Eleven

. . . .

Relationship Coaching

Coaching with regard to personal relationships is about helping Clients to get on with other people.

Not everyone has the natural skills to get on with others and this may arise for a number of reasons.

For example, someone may have a tendency to behave so assertively that others regard them as aggressive and someone to avoid.

Or you may be someone who is unable to trust other people and this happens because you do not trust yourself.

Or you may be someone who has made bad choices in the past and who builds up a reference to this bad-decision making. You hold a self-limiting belief

"I *always make the wrong decision so I don't trust my own choices.*"

Consequently, you are unable to be completely open with others and have difficulty finding the partner of your dreams.

Using Emotional Intelligence To Enhance Your Relationships

Emotional intelligence is learning how to respond and never react to people, situations or events.

Nobody can make you feel bad, sad or happy - unless you give them permission to.

If you say to somebody *"this person annoys me,"* you are giving them permission to annoy you.

It comes back to personal responsibility and being very aware of your emotions.

Emotional intelligence is about exercising choice over how other people make you feel.

For example, somebody comes to your mind and you feel – *"I like being in this person's company because I always laugh a lot and feel good."*

Or somebody comes to your mind and you feel – "You drive me mad."

In doing this you are allowing that person to drive you mad.

You need to learn how to tolerate this person, and in so doing, you are *making a choice* to tolerate this person.

This may be in relation to someone you have to live with e.g. if you lose your house and have to move in with someone you would prefer not to live with.

What you can do is set up boundaries and choose what you can and cannot tolerate.

In this scenario, this is the best move to take at the moment.

The person is not their behaviour.

Their behaviour relates to habits they have formed and experiences they have encountered over the years.

Difficult Relationships

When you are struggling with a family member or a parent, working on your relationship through emotional intelligence will help you accept them as they are, because nothing can change the fact, they are family.

To move forward, the first step is often forgiveness. You may be harbouring resentment towards the person for some past harm. You need to think of this person in terms of separating their behaviour from who they are.

For example, when you look at your father solely as your father or your mother solely as your mother – this makes you feel differently about them; because generally with your mother and father it is natural to think, *he is my father/she is my mother, so of course I love them.*

Once you can separate their identity from their behaviour, there is freedom. By making room for forgiveness, and moving towards a frame of mind where you think – "*I can never accept what they did, however I accept them as my parents/siblings,*". *You* can then handle the relationship differently.

It is about becoming very aware of how you relate to someone and how you react to them.

If someone approaches you in an aggressive or negative way, you have a choice on how to respond and to think about the dynamics of what is happening in the present.

What you want to avoid is passive or aggressive behaviour. Instead you want to be assertive in your relationships.

You think along the lines of "*I am my own observer* "and in so doing you can stop any escalation in what you observe.

For example, if you take a step back to observe how you are feeling and realise you are starting to become angry, you can take a moment to pause and then choose to stop becoming angry.

Over time you can develop this skill so that you are always in control of your behaviour.

It is all about acceptance, which replaces resentment and reminding yourself that the person you are interacting with is not their behaviour.

CASE STUDY

EMOTIONAL BULLYING

The female partner in a relationship came to seek coaching because she felt she was living in a prison and could not continue. After providing the client with relevant questions to work on, she reported back that her partner was not willing to participate in the coaching.

It turned out he did not share her values and was in fact bullying and gas lighting her. He did this by talking over her, shouting her down, telling her at regular intervals that she didn't know what she was talking about.

She also said that the atmosphere in the home all depended on the humour her partner was in at any given time. If he was in bad mood she felt she was walking on eggshells. Because she never knew what mood he would be in when she went home, she dreaded going home.

What brought the situation to breaking point was when her young son started repeating her husband's behaviour by addressing her in derogatory terms. One day in conversation with her son, he suddenly blurted, 'Sure what would you know anyway?' That was the day she decided she was leaving the relationship.

The couple went on to decide they did not share the same values in life and so they broke up.

Following the break-up of the relationship, I continue to coach this client around her own self-worth and building up her self-esteem. Gradually she started to own her own power again.

The Elements That Make Up A Relationship

There are four important aspects to every relationship:

❖ Physical
❖ Mental
❖ Emotional
❖ Spiritual

A problem in relation to any of the four areas can break up a relationship.

For example, if someone is physically beaten by their partner, or mentally and emotionally drained by them, they will either leave the relationship or be broken by it.

It is also worth bearing in mind that relationships grow, develop and change as time goes on.

For example, when you are young, the physical and emotional side of your relationship is very high in value, but when grow older, most of the time, it is the spiritual side that grows.

What this means is, you tend to put more importance on companionship and having someone to go places with and enjoy breaks away with, than you do on the physical side of your relationship.

Physical Side Of A Relationship

As long as there is a spark between parties in a relationship there is always a chance to rekindle that spark even when the relationship is in trouble.

However if there was no spark to begin with, how can you ever hope to light a spark in the first instance?

The reality is all relationships and marriages do not come about as a result of love. Some couples may be thrown together and get married because it is convenient to do so.

In such an arrangement however, the relationship can decline over time.

When the couple eventually take the opportunity to look back on how they came together, they may realise they were never emotionally or physically attracted to each other. The chances of them staying together in the long term, would therefore be most unlikely.

It can happen that both parties in a relationship are not aware that the cause of their problems was that there was never a spark between them.

Through coaching however, they can quickly come to realise their reality, and develop tools to move forward in their life.

CASE STUDY

A mother sent her young son to me for coaching.

He wanted to change his surname because he hated his father and was being bullied at school.

I coached this young man through exercises that empowered him to learn how to stand up for himself and value himself as a person. We also worked on his relationship with himself and his father in a pro-active way.

A number of years later the mother came to me for coaching herself, telling me:

'I stayed in a marriage because of tradition for the sake of my children. I stayed with a man I did not love and I have seen the damage it caused my children'.

'I am now ready to see you because I am ready to leave this man.'

The woman had witnessed the changes in her sons brought about through coaching and as we worked together to build up her own self-esteem and confidence, she went on to leave her husband and start a new life.

This case highlights the fact that families often stay together based on traditional beliefs and financial circumstances, even when parties are very unhappy in the relationship which effects everyone involved in a negative way.

Mental Side Of A Relationship

We attract what we believe we are.

Someone who enjoys intelligent discussion, books, reading etc. will not be attracted to a person who does not engage in debate or discussion. They will need someone who challenges them.

In a relationship where the mental/intellectual part of their relationship may not hold as much importance as the physical and spiritual side they too can be happy, once they share the same values.

Emotional Side Of A Relationship

Your partner and you both need to be able to satisfy each other's emotional needs in a relationship, which includes meeting both your desires for affection and intimacy.

If you or your partner do not offer emotional support to each other, then the emotional side of your relationship will be lacking.

Spirit Side Of A Relationship

Your values are reflected in what you want to do in life and what you wish to spend time on and who you want to spend your time with.

Once your values match those of your partner, you can be helped through difficult times to rebuild your relationship.

Tuning into your shared values will allow your relationship to continue to flourish and grow.

However, if one party places a higher value on something that the other partner is not interested in, if there is no compromise, the couple can eventually separate.

What Attracts One Person To Another Mentally?

Generally there are three types of people attracted to each other:

1.   Opposite Temperaments

2.   Similar Temperaments

3.   Opposite Temperaments and similar Values.

Opposite Temperaments

Sometimes, someone with a very outgoing personality who is perhaps very visual, would be attracted to a detailed, calm person.

Opposites attract, however can such a relationship stand the test of time? – That's the key question.

Typically in a relationship based on opposite temperaments, the couple go through an in-love period that may last in or around fifteen months.

This is a time when both partners think and feel they are in love with each other, until, one day they wonder -

"Where to from here? Where are we going from here?"

This is a crucial test moment in the relationship and unless these two people with the *opposite temperaments* want the same values in life, it is likely that they will separate.

For example, let's say in one such couple, one partner wants to live in the country but the other wants to stay in the city.

A pull-push momentum will start to build where the partners will struggle around thoughts of *"should I stay or should I go."*

In this scenario, where the couple could not compromise on their value of where to live, it will be most likely the reason that the relationship will end.

Similar Temperaments

Where a partner chooses a partner with a similar temperament, they may be settling for someone the same as themselves.

They are deciding:

"I want someone who sees the world and filters information in the same way as I do."

Because of the sameness between them, these couples may well be the ones you observe in a restaurant who have nothing to talk about because they tend to filter information the same way and think the same way. Therefore they can become bored with each other.

Nonetheless partners with similar temperaments can stay together because they share the same personal and core values.

Opposite Temperaments And Same Values

In this type of relationship one partner may be calm and detailed, while the other is outgoing and visual as in the first example, but in terms of their values they may have the same dreams and plans for their life.

Because they see things differently however, they can also grow together and learn from each other and challenge each other.

Once they have the same plans for life, the chances are they can have a very sustainable, loving, enjoyable and fulfilling relationship.

Know Your Values, Know Yourself

You must know what you want to attract into your life.

Most people who share the same top three personal and core values stay together.

Once you know your top three personal and core values you will be very clear about what you want to attract in.

If you do not know the values you want in a partner, you may simply drift in and out of relationships.

CASE STUDY

PARTNERS WHO HAD DIFFERENT VALUES

An example where a difference in values occurred in a relationship.

A couple came for coaching, who had both agreed that their top value was to invest and redecorate their home.

Soon, the husband got a promotion and as a result, he worked very long hours. He would arrive home late in the evening. His wife missed him desperately, but he would only say, 'stop complaining, I'm bringing home more money.'

In effect what had happened was that his values had changed through his thinking. He now placed his top core value on his career, and wanted to spend more time at work. There was an obvious shift in his value system, but it was only on one side.

I was able to empower the couple through coaching, to see what had happened. He had become completely caught up in his job and while his partner was supporting him through his promotion, the consequences was she was feeling very lonely and left behind.

I encouraged them to revisit a time where they both valued each other's company and was happy.

Fortunately, their love was strong enough and both were agreeable to finding a resolution to the situation. It was clear both parties needed to make a compromise. His wife continued supporting him in his Career and he resolved the problem by reducing the number of promotions he attended, and spent more time in their lovely home.

Exercise For Relationships

Identifying Your Personal Values And Those Of Your Partner

Describe what you don't want in a relationship.

List your top 10 personal values in a relationship.

Now prioritise your top 10 personal values into the top 3.

Look at your existing relationship with your significant other and with one previous relationship as well. In each relationship, list your present and previous partner's top 10 personal values.

Now compare their personal values to your top 3.

NOTE:

The point of this exercise is to identify exactly what you want and what you do not want in a relationship.

It requires you to identify your top 10 personal values and those you would want *your significant other* to have. You then prioritise your top 10 values to your top 3 personal values.

CASE STUDY

In the case of one client who had been in a relationship for seven years, she listed her top three personal and core values. I asked her did they match those of her partner, she said they did not.

This was because while he matched two of her top personal values of integrity and honesty, one of her core values was to get married and have a family, however she realised it was not one of his core values.

Following our coaching session, she said she would go home and continue the exercise with her partner. She invited him to make a list of his top 10 personal and core values.

She found her partner was agreeable to do the exercise and both looked over each other's list of personal and core values.

When she stated family and children as a core value on her list, her partner replied:

"I have been waiting for the moment to discuss this with you. I do not share these same core values."

When she asked him to expand on what he was saying, he said –

"I do not want the same core values as you, family, and children. I was waiting and waiting to tell you, but it was never the right time to bring this up."

While the revelation was a dreadful shock to the client, at least it meant she was now able to make some decisions and move forward. Having got the opportunity to tell her the truth, her partner moved on and the relationship ended.

How To Meet Your Ideal Partner?

If you do nothing to help yourself meet the partner of your dreams, nothing will happen.

You cannot stay at home and wait for *Mr Right* because *Mr Right* is simply not going to come knocking on your door.

It is always about doing something to get the process moving!!!

You must also know what you want and focus on it in a relationship.

If you want someone with a positive attitude to life but find yourself with a partner who is not of such a disposition, the relationship cannot thrive.

For example, a client was with a partner who she noted treated other people badly and with no respect. His life seemed to be all about playing the victim and arguing that everyone else had it easier than him.

Having decided to leave the relationship, I coached this client to empower her to find the right partner by helping her identify the right places to meet people who would share her personal and core values.

If you want to meet someone with particular interests, obviously you would look to meet them in the places where they can enjoy these interests.

For example, if you don't want to meet someone who spends their time in a pub, don't go to the pub!

Unfortunately a lot of the social culture in Ireland is around pubs, but this changes as you get older. Many people enjoy spending time going out for a meal with friends or partners.

Of course, it can still happen that you meet your true love in a pub, but if you want to meet someone who enjoys hill-walking then the best place to meet them would be to go hill-walking with friends or a local group.

Once you start going out more often to places you like, you will attract people of similar energy to you. People who have shared values and like to do the same things, will naturally come together in places of common interest.

If you really enjoy the outdoors and keeping fit and healthy, outdoor pursuits are where you are going to meet people with similar interests.

Obviously if you have a hobby you are passionate about, the chances are that in pursuing your hobby, you will discover common ground with someone and find that your values are similar.

The key is to socialise in places with people of common interest.

Affirmations To Help You Meet Your Soul Mate

Affirmations can be extremely useful in terms of finding the course of true love.

There is so much proof that affirmations work and in relationship coaching I have seen this happen again and again.

All around my office I have thousands of beautiful *"thank you"* cards from people who have met the partner they wanted.

For example, one woman who employed an affirmation based around meeting someone who reflected her top three personal and core values, reported that she had met someone special who shared her top three personal and core values.

They are now very happy together and expecting their first child.

Exercise

Forming Affirmations To Meet Your True Love

In order to form an affirmation to help you meet your partner in life you must first of all identify your top three personal values.

Now, form an affirmation around these and after that just let it go and allow life to happen. An example of an affirmation here could be:

I am now attracting into my life a man who I share a spark with, who has a positive attitude to life and who is generous.

This affirmation contains three top personal values and all the person has to do is to say it several times during the day and then just relax and let it become a reality.

Relationship Breakdown

Relationships break down for two main reasons:

1. Lack of communication.

2. Conflict in values.

In relation to a conflict in values, it is worth noting that it can take time to discover shared values, as a person's values show through in different situations as people develop in the relationship.

Therefore, it takes time to get to know somebody and for example, while a person may clearly be generous when it comes to paying for your meal together, you will still need to give time to see if they are generous with their emotional support.

Similarly it will take time to discover another person's philosophy on life and how they react when things go against them. These are things you can only learn as time goes on.

The Four R's That Can Destroy A Relationship

When you are unhappy in a relationship, emotion escalates and the following happens:

Resistance begins

Resentment sets in

Rejection follows

Repression of emotions occurs i.e. there is no passion.

Where barriers arise in a relationship there is still hope for the future if you love each other enough to compromise on certain values.

Then the relationship can continue.

You Attract In What You Believe Yourself

Relationships can be formed on the basis of what has gone before.

For example, you might have a pattern from past relationships where your thinking around shared happiness with a partner is that it is something that cannot last.

You are operating from a self-limiting belief that *"this is too good to last"*, and ultimately, thinking about your relationship this way will manifest this as a reality and the relationship inevitably ends.

In your past history where you experience your Dad having been unfaithful to your Mum it might carry through to a belief in your own thinking around relationships and you think and believe: *"All men will treat me badly* and *all men are unfaithful."*

But the past reality of previous relationships is not a predictor of future realities.

If your belief centres around thinking *"there are bad men out there,"* of course we know this statement may be true, but it cannot be applied in terms of men in general.

Again, the use of affirmations in situations where self-limiting beliefs hold you back can be very beneficial.

For example, where the self-limiting belief around men arose from the Dad being unfaithful to the Mum, a useful affirmation to repeat on a daily basis would be:

"There are lovely men out there and I am attracting into my life, a man I share a spark with, who I trust and who is faithful to me."

CASE STUDY ON SELF-LIMITING BELIEF

A client who came to me for relationship coaching, revealed a self-limiting belief around not being deserving of long-term happiness.

I worked with the client to change their mindset through forming an affirmation that moved her away from these thoughts.

The affirmation focused instead on placing the client in the mindset of being in a relationship she could enjoy on a day-to-day basis for the long term.

The idea was to have her believe this had already happened in her life.

The affirmation was as follows:

"I am in a relationship, and day by day it is getting better and better."

Anger Management In Relationships

If a client comes to me with an anger problem in regard to a particular area in their relationship, I can go no further unless the client is willing to explore where this anger originates from and what are the triggers.

In the world of relationships, you are who you are today, because of what you have accepted up to now and you must take personal responsibility for that.

If someone is treating you badly it is because *you are allowing them to treat you this way.*

When somebody comes to me and says they are in a painful relationship, I ask:

"Who is allowing this person to do, say or behave this way?"

The client then realises it is themselves who is allowing it.

I then ask:

"Can you accept that it is you who is allowing this?"

At first, the client pauses and attempts to lay the blame on the other person.

They say, if I had more money or if I had not met this person, my life would be perfect.

Basically they are trying to blame the world and other people for where they are today, when the reality is they are where they are, because of the choices they have made.

Relationships are all about taking *'personal responsibility.'*

You must take personal responsibility for your life and your choices.

Money Is The Key

It is my experience that money is one of the major reason for relationships breaking down. I believe it is the highest factor that affects relationship as money affects power which in turn affects love.

During the recession, I was coaching a lot of people in relationship difficulty where one partner lost their job and their power. The coaching was around what they could do to bring equal power back to the relationship.

Where a change of circumstance occurs a partner can suddenly feel dependent on the other person in the relationship. There is a loss of independence and coaching helps to work through this.

Typically in this kind of coaching I would ask each person to answer the question, *"How powerful do you feel now?"*

This opens their mind to the main issue that needs to be worked on, through compromise and support for each other.

The sense of powerlessness and lack of independence, a person can suddenly feel in their relationship, following the change in their own circumstances, needs to be communicated, acknowledged, discussed, and dealt with.

Even just to say *"things are going to be different now* and *we will deal with it as it is happening"* shows an acknowledgement of the situation and an agreement to work through it.

Couples must accept where they are at and be willing to find their way through as part of their continuing journey together.

Failing to do so will mean they are living in denial by avoiding the elephant in the room.

Communication Issues Between Partners

While a psychological contract may exist in a work environment, where you may be expected to do tasks that were never communicated to you verbally - this psychological contract also exists in a personal relationship where you assume that your partner knows exactly what you are thinking without communicating verbally.

For example, a client once told me that her partner knew it drove her mad when he left his clothes thrown all over the bedroom floor instead of putting them into the laundry basket. I asked when she had told him that it irritated her and she stared blankly at me.

The reality was she had never said it to him. She just assumed he knew it annoyed her. Of course he would continue to do it until it was brought to his attention. Once she communicated verbally to him the annoyance of his habit, he quickly corrected the problem.

People who live together become moulded in their behaviours, and familiar in their thinking while living with each other. Sometimes they assume that each other knows what goes on in the other person's mind.

The reality is that where a partner has an unpleasant personal habit, you must communicate it to the person and share the impact this habit has on you in the first instance.

How else can they know it annoys you?

Fall Out From Poor Communication

Regardless of how you are feeling, communication is paramount in relationships.

Communicating with your partner is about understanding each other and how you see things differently in life.

When people do not talk about what they are feeling, and what has happened in their day, this is when problems happen in their relationship.

The biggest breakdown occurs when trust is broken and this can come about through a loss of communication.

While it is possible to rekindle a relationship after trust has broken down, it takes a very long time to re-build trust and this can only happen through tiny steps being taken one at a time.

For example, if someone had an affair, they might discover that their partner is someone who has a high value around fidelity.

However, if they were lucky enough that their partner still wanted them back – even after the affair, they could work towards repairing their relationship by re- building trust between them, one small step at a time.

The reason a partner may be open to continuing in a relationship after an affair is entirely connected to their values.

Most people who commit to each other in marriage do so with the intention of staying together forever.

However, there are definitely some who marry for different reasons and who do not share their partner's values regarding fidelity.

Before anyone goes to the stage of having an affair, there is generally a breakdown in the two main areas; lack of communication and a conflict in values.

The third area of contention can relate to where a power change happens in the relationship because of money.

For a relationship to be sustainable and lasting, there must be an equal power share.

What Relationship Coaching Involves

Where a couple presents for coaching, they are coached separately as opposed to being coached together at the beginning.

Initially, a profile assessment is carried out which entails conducting individual temperament assessment with each person.

Many people would not have completed a profile assessment before, and would not have taken the time to try and understand how the other person thinks and behaves.

Some people will do anything to avoid conflict and so they remain passive until a situation escalates and it gets too much for them.

At this point they may explode at their partner in the presence of others, when really they could have resolved the problem in an earlier discussion in private.

Sometimes the cause of the conflict can be external.

For example, you may want to ask your boss for a wage increase but find you haven't the confidence. You then go home angry with yourself and take your aggression out on the person in your life, your partner.

Personality and temperament profiling is a very important and a useful element in relationship coaching.

As part of the profiling process, individual values are also discussed. When both parties come together, they realise that everyone can view the world in different ways, however not necessarily through conflict. It is about understanding, valuing different perspectives and respecting the differences in each other.

In the relationship coaching, the couple will talk and decide either that they are willing to compromise and work together on any difference in values between them or, as one man attending coaching once stated, "*I am not going to compromise on the value I place on my work* ", which literally translated some weeks later into- *"our relationship is over."*

While these words in that coaching session were indeed shocking, the reality is the coach never tells a couple what to do.

Both parties instead, arrive at their own answers, then make their decisions and choices, taking full ownership for what they choose to do.

CASE STUDY - UNCOVERING SELF-LIMITING BELIEFS WHICH DAMAGED A RELATIONSHIP

A woman who was at a high achieving point in her career was unsure of her current relationship and did not know whether she wanted to commit to marrying her partner or not.

In the first coaching session with this client, we took a helicopter look at her life, taking time to consider her home life, her career, how much time she spent with her loved one – who in this instance was also in a demanding job.

We completed the Wheel of Life exercise in relation to all areas of her life, assessing which were high and low.

In the area of money we found that she was very happy with the amount she had in her life because she was in fact quite wealthy.

However, she also felt quite low about her money situation in regard to relationships. This was based on a self-limiting beliefs and long-standing fears she held that "people used her for her money."

These beliefs had led her to believe that maybe her partner was only with her because of her money.

When asked to provide examples of where she felt this was evident, it transpired she could not provide any concrete examples.

This line of questioning revealed that quite the opposite was true and that her partner loved her and would love her – even if she didn't have any money.

Given this discovery we then needed to ascertain where her sense of distrust was coming from.

The client went on to reveal that in the past her friends and family had used her to make money for them.

Immediately I was able to point out to her that she had carried this self-limiting belief from the past to where she was now. She still believed that people were only with her for her money and it was this belief that was now destroying her relationship with someone she loved.

We then looked at the client's past, and I invited my client to learn from her experiences and to forgive the person responsible for her forming these self-limiting beliefs.

We continued to work on building up her self-esteem and to focus only on attracting people who wanted and accepted her for who she was.

At the end of this first session, we also discovered that the client was not emotionally attracted to her partner, because neither of them told the other how they felt for each other emotionally.

We also discovered that their difficulties came down to trust – and trust is the salvation of every relationship.

She didn't trust her partner even though he had given her no reason not to trust him.

Her mistrust was due to a self-limiting belief.

DELVING DEEPER INTO THE RELATIONSHIP

After developing some affirmations for the client to work through on her self- limiting belief around money, over the remaining coaching sessions we delved deeper into the area of their personal relationship, looking at the four important aspects for consideration.

As a result of this, we discovered that there was a discrepancy between both parties regarding the emotional and spiritual sides of their relationship.

Coaching therefore centred on working through their differences in these areas.

PHYSICAL

In order to examine the physical side of the relationship I asked the Client:

> *Describe to me what you see when you bring your partner to mind; do you like what you see?*

The client informed me that when she brought her partner to mind she did like what she saw and therefore confirmed that the physical side of the relationship was good.

EMOTIONAL

We looked at the area of their emotional relationship and how the client felt her partner responded to her emotional needs.

After putting some questions to the client around this, she revealed that she felt her partner offered her little emotional support or intimacy.

There were no hugs and she did not feel he was there for her emotionally.

This line of questioning therefore exposed the emotional side of the relationship as questionable.

MENTAL

Regarding the mental side of the relationship, I discovered that the client felt satisfied in this area and that both partners challenged each other mentally in a positive way.

SPIRITUAL

Exploring the spiritual side of the relationship, I asked the client did she feel, she and her partner were figuratively walking the way forward together with the same plans and values.

To this she stated that there was a discrepancy here. Her partner wanted to move the relationship to the next level of commitment i.e. marriage but she was not sure she could agree to this with someone who she believed was not giving her emotional support.

She also disclosed she had been very hurt when she discovered that her partner had confided in a friend and said he felt perhaps he was wasting his time in his relationship with her.

The friend reported this back to the client and it had a big impact on her.

I asked the client to consider the following:

Do you really love this person?

She said all she could say was she felt pushed into a corner, where he wanted her to marry him, but she believed at this time, he was not the person she had fallen in love with.

At this point the client's partner agreed to come for coaching.

We spoke about the situation and on the matter of making a lifetime commitment I coached him into realising that he should not give his partner an ultimatum because generally when this happens, the partner will leave the relationship.

I coached him into the reality that you never get what you want in life if you chase it, so the best approach would be for him to go back to being his funny natural self and to just live and enjoy the relationship every day.

To help him act in this way we worked together to form some affirmations to incorporate into his day that included:

"I am in a beautiful and intimate relationship."

"I live in the now and enjoy every minute of our relationship."

Four months later the woman was proposed to in a hot air balloon and declared:

Yes, I've got back the man I fell in love with.

Long Term Relationships

Many people in long-term relationships have questions around where the relationship is going and whether they should stay or go.

Coaching them through this involves posing a number of questions which make them reflect on their relationship, such as the following:

Are you happy in your relationship?

Do you want the same values in life?

Often Clients say at this point, 'I never thought of it like that.'

What they realise now is, they are now at a stage of wanting to move to the next level, often to have children. All around them they see friends getting married and starting families but nothing seems to be happening for them.

I provide some further questions to consider, such as:

Have you ever talked to your partner about this?

Very often women tell me that when this topic comes up with their partner, the partner fobs off the question or ducks and dives in order to avoid facing up to it.

They say things like, *we can deal with this later,* but then they never do and the clock ticks on.

Letting Things Slide

People in relationships often just let things go. They let things slide.

They fob each other off with platitudes such as: *"when we're married for years we can talk again about children, or sure aren't we grand the way we are?"*

What both parties here are doing is avoiding the issue, procrastinating, and not truthfully communicating.

The reality is that some people just do not want to commit; and some have a fear of commitment.

It is more common than people imagine, that one wants to marry and the other doesn't. It is sometimes not discussed.

If you do not want to compromise on your core values – which in this instance relates to committing to a partner/marriage for life - the chances are your relationship will break up.

Twelve

· ·

My Secrets And Tips To A Happy And Fulfilling Life

As a Personal & Executive Coach who loves her work, I wish to share with you my secrets to a happy and fulfilling life.

I am where I am today because of my mindset which has helped me manifest the life of my dreams.

Too often, I have witnessed people giving up on life too easily. I believe life is precious and I would never give up on it.

I am a Personal & Executive Coach who trained and qualified people to be coaches as well as living the life of a coach. Learning is immense because we are dealing with real life stories.

As one of the first coaches in Ireland, I have trained and qualified over 400 people to work as coaches and I believe there will be much more development in this field.

Because the training involves so much interaction and personal investment, people readily remember what they have learned and can go on to apply it to real life.

As a Master Practitioner in Neuro -Linguistic Programming, which is a powerful tool, along with Emotional Intelligence, it allows me go into the world of the client and hear the language they are using to share their experiences.

I find my work most fulfilling and I am very passionate about it. People come to me confused and lost, but leave with a goal or a set of goals to achieve. When a client leaves a session, both the client and I experience the powerful process of coaching.

I use meditation/mindfulness following a coaching session to relax.

In addition to coaching people, I go into companies to work with personnel on performance improvement. I diligently apply my coaching skills into my own daily work, to be productive and achieve my very best each day.

In 2000 I trained in the United States to be a Coach under the excellent tutelage of Thomas J Leonard, who set up "Coach U" in 1997.

My mission is to reach millions of people to empower them to realise they can manifest what they want in life and it is all about choice.

I would like my legacy to be that I empowered others to be the best they could be, while always remaining true to their values and moving from great to brilliant. This is my purpose.

Share Your Talents And Passion In Order To Live A Fulfilling Life

You are not meant to hide your talents. Within all of us we have talents and gifts to share.

You must focus on sharing your talents in a passionate way with others around you because their world will thrive and benefit from them.

Success Means Taking Personal Responsibility

Respect your time and get up a half hour earlier so that you can have a relaxed breakfast and get ready for your day.

Be present to everyone you share your life with.

Move gently through your morning rituals, no rushing and fussing.

Don't do anything that causes you stress.

Do not allow room for chaos.

Avoid stressful queues and traffic by going to the shops at quiet times and avoiding rush hour when travelling.

Value other people's time and make sure you always turn up for engagements with a few minutes to spare if possible.

If someone is causing you stress, do not spend so much time with them.

It is all a choice.

You always have a choice.

Every single thought is energy and this energy can be positive or negative.

Behind every decision lies your value system.

It is not possible to get it right every time, because life gets in the way, but whatever causes you stress, make the effort to deal with it or move away from it.

Developing good habits around how you get up and get ready each day will give you a head start.

Success means different things to different people.

For some it could mean living in a beautiful house - for others it is about when happiness and fulfilment come from the inside.

Be responsible for yourself and be proud of what you believe in. It is about being proud of who you are and then living in alignment with your values. This allows you to be at peace with yourself and everyone else.

Be true to yourself and have unconditional love and self-acceptance, because we cannot love anyone else unless we love ourselves first.

Accept and forgive yourself for any negative choices you have made in the past and deal with issues as they arise.

Do not live in past realities as this can affect you in the now. Be in the moment and take personal responsibility for where you are. In taking personal responsibility you will enjoy tranquillity, peace and relaxation.

Where you are not true to your value system internally, you will always encounter conflict.

This can happen where you make a decision to stay with the wrong person; or feel you are a prisoner in your own home; or staying in the wrong profession or job.

Move away from procrastination and be more proactive.

Maintain a work life balance.

Ensure you have enough quality time with friends and family, so that you have no regrets when you leave this world.

Live your life to the full.

Where you make a mistake, stop, evaluate, reflect, and then move on with the learning.

This is success.

Manage Your Time Wisely And Be Organised

In your life it is vital that you manage your time.

Managing your time means you are also managing your stress.

Be organised so that your life is not all about chasing from one thing to the next.

How I Manage My Own Time?

As a Personal & Executive Coach, I live my life as I encourage others to do.

I am always on time from a time-management perspective, and I am respectful of other people's time.

I am an early morning riser and as a result my energy is very high in the morning.

When I go to the gym, it is early in the morning.

Managing and valuing my time means I avoid procrastination.

When I meet with friends, we forward plan our next outing, while everyone is together and have their diaries with them.

Treating your time in this way shows you place a high value on it.

At weekends I like to be with family and friends and enjoy being at home.

Spending quality time doing what I want, refreshes and re-boots my energy for the following week.

Sundays Are For Family And Friends

I never work on a Sunday.

I always take Sundays off to spend time with my family/friends or just to be.

We all need a day when we stop "doing."

We are human *"beings"* not human *"doings"*.

We are meant to *"be"* in the moment more than we are.

We spend so much of our time *"doing"* we find it difficult to take time to just *"be"*.

The Benefits Of Managing Stress

Because I manage my life so purposefully I do not bring stress on myself.

This is how I choose to live because I would not be able to live a life that is all about rushing.

Of course stressful situations will always arise, because we cannot control everything that happens around us.

However when stressful situations arise, I rationalise them.

For example, if there was a traffic delay and I was going to be late for a meeting, rather than stress out about it I would communicate my difficulty to the person I was to meet, accept the inevitable and get through the wait by listening to relaxing music.

I would then arrive very calmly into the meeting and apologise for the delay. Again it is a matter of choice. You can choose to allow stress to build or you can choose to remain calm and manage how you feel and act.

Stress is about "feeling out of control" and anxiety is "the false stories we tell ourselves about the future that frightens us." They arise when you feel out of control because of having to deal with a situation you were not prepared for.

Stress will come and go but how you manage it is what counts.

If you can remain emotionally calm it need not interfere with the smooth running of your life.

Be Yourself And Do Not Live In A World Of Comparisons

In my coaching work I come across all kinds of people but most fall into two groups.

1.

There are those who live in "*the now*" and enjoy every minute of life as it happens.

2.

There are others who spend much of their time looking around at how the rest are living their lives and comparing themselves to them.

You either live in the world of "*now*" or the world of "*comparisons*".

In the land of comparisons you are always comparing yourself to other people and wondering what they are thinking about you. This means you are out of control because you are allowing your energy to go to other people.

People who live in the land of comparison tend to be perfectionists, but seeking perfectionism is not positive. It is having a false feeling about how great you are and is very connected to the ego. It also creates a line in the sand to say that nobody can jump any higher than this line.

When you go into this world, you are serving the other person's beliefs and not your own. Once your energy goes into comparing yourself to others you cannot focus your energy on yourself. The only time you can be your best is when you focus on yourself.

When I coach people in this area I might say, *"I know you want to be a star and to give your best, but who are you comparing yourself to?"*

When they reflect on this for a while I give them the analogy of bees in a jar – where someone puts a lid on the jar. Some bees will jump half way, some jump to the lid but if you take the lid off, some bees will jump even higher.

There is always going to be somebody who is going to achieve more and jump over that line, however what is important is to move away from comparing and just focus on you being your best.

Believe in abundance and do not worry about other people setting up in competition to you because there is room out there for everyone.

Be your best and give your best at any moment in time.

Stop comparing yourself to other people as this is the fastest route to failure.

Focusing on what other people are doing is draining and can create doubts in our head about ourselves.

Living in a world of comparisons also creates some self-limiting beliefs in our head about ourselves.

Move out of the effect of this and into control.

None of us has the right to say what is best but you can control how you think and behave by being your own best.

We all know and recognise people who give their best. If you are someone who gives your best you will always keep your standards high.

This gives you more freedom to explore and grow your own mind.

I come from a place where I love and accept myself and always give my best.

In return, I trust people to receive the best from me and in practice I know this to be true because it is evident in the feedback I receive.

My energy is always focused on how I can give more and be of service to others.

Affirmations I Use To Empower Me To Live A Positive Life

I have strong affirmations that I say to myself on a daily basis to help me stay strong and positive.

Some of the affirmations I use are as follows:

I am a strong, powerful and loving person

I can achieve what I want in life

I only focus on what I can do something about

I live a wonderful life and give a wonderful service

My intention is always about — 'how can I serve you today?'

Overcoming Moments When Life Gets You Down

On occasions, when I feel let down, I allow myself a few moments to wallow and then move to what I can do something about.

Rather than panicking, if you find yourself in such circumstances, stay calm and view your situation from the perspective of what you have power over.

What can you do about something?

I have found thinking in this way to be one of my greatest strengths.

Because I view life in a positive way, I always look for the beauty in people. That comes from a time when I was very young and attended Church as a teenager to listen to the priests who visited from the missions.

I remember one priest who said, "*If you look for the good in people you will find it, and if you look for the bad in people you will also find it.*" – "*Choose what you look for.*"

I have looked for the beauty in people ever since and 99% of the time I find it.

Some Final Words To Help Smooth Your Journey In Life

The following are some final words I wish to share to empower you to live a wonderful life:

Use your gifts and follow your passion.

You manifest exactly what you focus on.

What other people think of you is none of your business, so accept and love yourself.

When you are thinking in terms of "*what if*" about something negative that may happen in the future, don't allow it to depress you. Instead, use the words "*what if*" as a motivator for the best thing that could happen and focus on that.

You cannot undo the past, you can only learn from it and take the learning as a positive into your future.

Everyone gets the same 24 hours per day, so value your time and ensure you enjoy a work/life balance.

Whenever you are asked to do something, do an internal check on your value system and how the request makes you feel. Saying *yes* to something is saying *no* to something else. When you do say *no*, don't apologise or get defensive. Be polite and make it a priority to value your time.

People notice when you become proactive. They sit up and take notice when changes are happening.

I trust that you have found some coaching tips and tools that have enlightened and inspired you from this book.

Always remember to listen to your inner voice and your intuition. Please also listen to the voice of those around you who love and cherish you. As my book says – "Life begins when you are ready to listen".

Milton Keynes UK
Ingram Content Group UK Ltd.
UKHW022013011223
433643UK00011B/1140